DATE DUE

DE 19 '01			
FE 4 '02			
AG 8 02			
AP 03 '04			
JE 1 '04			
MY 31 '05			
JE 8 '05			
NO 1 6 '07			
DE 7 '07			
JE 1 7 '19			

DEMCO 38-296

RAISING
MULTILINGUAL CHILDREN

RAISING MULTILINGUAL CHILDREN

Foreign Language Acquisition and Children

Tracey Tokuhama-Espinosa

BERGIN & GARVEY
Westport, Connecticut • London

Library of Congress Cataloging-in-Publication Data

Tokuhama-Espinosa, Tracey, 1963–
    Raising multilingual children : foreign language acquisition and children /
  Tracey Tokuhama-Espinosa.
        p.   cm.
    Includes bibliographical references and index.
    ISBN 0–89789–750–1 (alk. paper)
    1. Bilingualism in children.   2. Child rearing.   3. Language
    acquisition.   4. Language and languages—Study and teaching.   5. English
    language—Study and teaching—Foreign speakers.   6. Comparative
    education.   I. Title.
  P115.2.T65   2001
    404'.2'083—dc21   00–029258

British Library Cataloguing in Publication Data is available.

Library of Congress Catalog Card Number: 00–029258
ISBN: 0–89789–750–1

First published in 2001

Bergin & Garvey, 88 Post Road West, Westport, CT 06881
An imprint of Greenwood Publishing Group, Inc.
www.greenwood.com

Printed in the United States of America

The paper used in this book complies with the
Permanent Paper Standard issued by the National
Information Standards Organization (Z39.48–1984).

10 9 8 7 6 5 4 3 2

In Appreciation

A warm hug of appreciation to my children, Natalie, Gabriel, and Mateo, and to Cristian for helping raise them, and a special thank you to my armchair linguist mother, Reba, and to my father and first teacher, Al.

And to all those who helped in the kitchen, foremost among them:

Dr. Cristina Allemann-Ghionda of Cologne University, Germany, and Dr. Terry Osborn of Queens College in New York for peerless peer advice.

Great appreciation is due to Jane Garry and David Palmer at Greenwood Publishing for their patience and guidance, and to Giselle Martínez de Meléndez, Cherise Valles McGivern, and Marlene Hall-Amsler who, in addition to being mothers of multilingual children, are careful and observant readers.

A very sincere thanks to Maureen O'Hanlon and her husband Jürgen Koch, Ulla Höhenwarter, Peggy Rodrigue, Mariana Quintero de Hugo, Corinne Kurz, Christine Tschabuschnig, Sarah Turney, Kim van Helvoort, Véronique Produit, Yolanda Ortoñes de García, and Galit Locker. You are greatly appreciated for your ideas, opinions, and stories.

Contents

Tables and Figures

_____ *Chapter 1* _____

The Search for the Secret to Successful Bilingualism: Somewhere between Academia and the Family

Before my first child was born I searched the local bookstores, picked the brains of friends with bilingual children, and scoured many a university library for information about raising children in a multilingual environment. My husband's first language is Spanish and mine is English, and I wanted to know the "secret" of successful bilingualism. I spoke about this issue with a great number of parents, pediatricians, and colleagues in Ecuador, Japan, Switzerland, France, and the United States and found different angles on this intriguing but often divisive issue of child development. In discussing bilingualism, the only common thread in many cases was the passion with which everyone would share their opinions on the subject. Aiding children to reach proficiency in two or more languages is an amazing mental feat; getting two families to agree on the right method is perhaps even more of a challenge. Many formulas seemed to work, but then again, there were so many different levels of proficiency in the children I observed that I began wondering about their true "success" as bilinguals. So I turned to more scholarly sources of information.

Each time I entered a new library I would typically begin my search in the "education" section where I found a good number of books about attempts at bilingual education *in the schools*, but not with respect to the parents' role. I would move on to my second academic love, and in the "psychology" section often found some things on self-esteem, gender differences, and sibling influences on language development, but mostly based on monolinguals and rarely mentioning bilingualism at all. Finally I would cross over into uncharted territory in my academic background and delve into the "medical" and "neurological" areas where I found information about brain structure and the cerebral mechanics of language processing, which were usually not intended for the average person's consumption.

All of these sources of information, both written, and in-the-flesh accounts, shed *some* light on *some* aspects of bilingual children, but nowhere did I find a simple, easy–to–read, factual account that addressed my needs as a parent and interests as a teacher. By the time I started my own writing I had two children with a third on the way and the question was not about bilingualism anymore, but about multilingualism, as we were adding a third language. So upon returning to Harvard University for a year while my husband worked on another degree, I began in earnest to research and write about the subject of multilingualism and children. I increased my knowledge related to neuropsychology by reading and taking courses in the field, and bolstered my understanding of the psychology of the written language, as well as studied the social aspects of language via courses in the anthropological aspect of cognition. I also encountered a great deal of new research in neurology and linguistics which backed up my own emerging theory, and excitedly began this project just after our move to Switzerland in 1998.

This is a book for parents, teachers, and caregivers of children who speak more than one language, or who want to do so. It is for scholars interested in cross-area studies within the cognitive sciences who are open to a theory of foreign language acquisition in children which comes from someone out of the academic loop, and within the experimental group being observed. It is about children like my daughter, Natalie, who was born in Ecuador to an Ecuadorian and an American. She began her life in Ecuador, then moved to the United States for a year, back to Ecuador briefly, and then to Switzerland by the time she was five years old. Children like her, and their families, experience a need to communicate in multiple languages in order to be functional members of society and to maintain consistencies in their family life. Though it may seem extraordinary at first glance, Natalie's story is not uncommon.

A NEW APPROACH FOR NEW TIMES

Thirty or forty years ago it was typical to think of those who lived abroad as missionaries, diplomats, or romantic expatriates. Now at the beginning of the new millenium, there are literally millions of families living abroad in this same linguistic boat. These families include the aforementioned traditional groups, but they also embrace a number of middle-class employees of large companies. Dupont, Microsoft, Xerox, Chevrolet, Arthur Andersen, Coca-Cola and IBM alone send tens of thousands of employees "abroad" with their families at some stage in their careers. The number of people in "foreign" countries is sky-rocketing given the reach of such multinational companies, the work of international organizations, and the expansion of foreign relations.

The new millenium brings with it a change of status afforded bilinguals who are now esteemed for their talent rather than shunned and deemed problematic, as was the case in the 1950s and 1960s in the United States' public schools (but which unfortunately still remains the case in some countries and educational systems around the world). More than ever, however, the ability to speak in other languages is increasingly seen as a desirable asset.

Three specific parent groups can be served by this book. It is for those families who work and live abroad and have filled the international schools' enrollments to overflowing: the Americans and other nationals who have "gone out" to join the international community. Secondly, it is for immigrants and other bilingual populations around the world and for the policy makers and teachers who serve them, a group that numbers in the millions in the United States alone. In 1980 there were 4.5 million school-age children in the United States who spoke a non-English language at home. In the early 2000s this could double. These are the new Americans who have just "come in" and whose task to assimilate includes the challenges of forming a new linguistic identity. And thirdly, this is a book for monolingual families who appreciate and value foreign languages as a useful tool for today's world and for today's minds. These are families that understand that speaking another language is a form of intelligence that gives their children a sophisticated view of the world, and which will serve them throughout their lives.

On the macro-level these three groups are distinct in that in the first case bilingualism or multilingualism is usually sought out by individual families trying to facilitate the usually temporary move to new surroundings. In the second case of immigrant populations, bilingualism or multilingualism is usually "imposed" by the local school system and societal pressure to integrate. There exists a difference in status afforded to the new ambassador in town compared with his immigrant counterpart as well. And in the third group, foreign language opportunities are also sought out, but not for survival purposes, but rather for their educational, social, and cultural benefits. However, on the micro-level these three groups are the same. When we discuss how individual children learn a new language it does not matter whether that person is a child of a Japanese diplomat arriving in Kenya, a Croatian immigrant coming to Switzerland, or the Smith family living in suburban California. In all three cases the children and their families face personal decisions and psychological challenges, and that is the focus of this book.

The first group of international expatriate families has created what is commonly referred to on the international school circuit as the *Third Culture Kids* syndrome (Pollock 1999). These are children who are born in a First Culture, attend school in a Second Culture, and live their daily life in a Third Culture. For example, Susan is an American who was born in the United States (Culture One). She attends school at the International School of the Sacred Heart (Culture Two) in Tokyo, and lives in Japan (Culture Three) due to her father's job. *Culture* here is broadly defined, to be sure, but the point is that Susan lives in three different "worlds" daily. She says she is an "American" but goes to school in a non-nationalistic, multi-religious, international environment and lives, sleeps, eats, plays, and socializes in Japan. Another example could be my daughter. She is half-Ecuadorian, half-American, who "was made in Japan," born in Ecuador, and is now attending the German School in French-speaking Geneva.

We as parents need guidance on how to flourish and not flounder in the midst of opportunity that mirrors mayhem. While the problems of cultural adjustment are real and important, the focus of this book is linguistic. And to this extent it addresses the second population as well: those new immigrants to the United States who are challenged by learning English as a Second Language and who wonder if they should maintain their own mother tongue at all. This book is meant to be a tool for integration. It is based on recent research

Each factor in raising multilingual children discussed in Chapters Three through Six is followed by true family profiles which bring life to our so-called kitchen, so that the importance of each ingredient or tool is easily understood.

Chapter Seven focuses on the roles of the Teacher and School when a child undertakes a foreign language. Is your child's current school curriculum sufficient? Should children living abroad learn to write in their native tongue or in that of the school system? What can teachers do to help the multilingual children in their lives? What "special handling" of the multilingual child needs to occur, if any? How different schools around the world approach the question of languages in the classroom and the vitally important role of teachers is shared in this chapter.

Chapter Eight is a chance for each parent to "bake their own" multilingual family, or in other terms, to evaluate their own situation in terms of the information just given. Using the Family Language Profile Worksheet, parents can see which "ingredient" has been missing, or which has been applied in excess, and learn how to modify the measurements to reap better language success. A discussion of the Degrees of Multilingualism follows, asking parents to reflect on their personal Family Language Goals. Do they want their child to be able to play with the neighbors? To pass first grade in their second language? To write proficiently in more than one language? To attend a university in another language? Depending on what the goals are, each family can better see what challenges and sacrifices they will have to make. If the goals include Multiliteracy Skills and the wide range of subjects that fall under this heading (from the differences between the spoken and written word, to how different school systems approach multiliteracy), then the last section of this chapter will prove to be worthwhile reading.

Chapter Nine addresses the great concern of many parents when faced with unsuccessful attempts at bilingualism. What can be done in problem situations? How can parents identify if their child has a speech problem or whether they have psychological difficulties related to their multilingualism? These questions and old biases against bilingualism are clarified. This chapter closes with some suggested reading lists divided into the areas of "Multilingualism in the Family," "Multiliteracy Skills," "Multilingual Education in the Schools," and "Brain Research and Multilingualism."

Chapter Ten summarizes the information presented in this book and offers diary entries from my own children's multilingual upbringing to illustrate all of the ingredients, baking instructions, and kitchen tools discussed in the rest of the book. Conclusions about the research-to-date are offered, and a final word will hopefully leave parents challenged to act with the information they have just been given.

_____ *Chapter 2* _____

Ten Key Factors in Raising Multilingual Children: A Recipe for Success

THREE REASONS WHY COOKING AND RAISING CHILDREN ARE THE SAME, AND ONE REASON WHY THEY ARE NOT

I love cooking. And I love my children. (Not necessarily in that order.) Both require a certain attention to detail, monitoring, and various ingredients to turn out right. Thousands upon thousands of general cookbooks have been written, and plenty of people will give you advice about rearing children. But when you get into specialty cooking, like fancy French desserts or vegetarian food delicacies, the selection narrows. And when you try to learn much more about very specific aspects of bringing up children, as in helping them in our fast-developing multilingual world, the selection is even more scarce. Cooking and raising children are the same in that each requires that you put something in (whether the ingredient is flour or love). Cooking and raising children are the same in that end results take awhile to achieve (a Russian Rum Baba dessert about an hour-and-a-half, our offspring eighteen years or more). And cooking and raising children are the same in that your finished product can make you feel rewarded a hundred-fold by your efforts, or you can be embarrassingly disappointed.

Cooking and raising children are very different when it comes to this last point, however. We can throw out the Rum Baba and begin again. We're stuck with the kid. Whereas the ingredients in your Rum Baba are replaceable, what you invest in your child's upbringing in terms of language development has an effect on his/her life forever. How can you be ensured of quality ingredients, of perfect timing, of good results?

A SAMPLING OF A SUCCESSFUL RECIPE

Evidence clearly points at certain "*do's*" and "*dont's*" when it comes to raising multilingual children. While the negative factors to avoid follow regular child rearing advice (don't mock a child when he has less than optimal success, for example), the positive factors need clarification in order to be applied properly. From a parent's perspective, what can be done to foster foreign language development in children?

Starting from Zero

Without scaring off well-intentioned mothers and fathers, I would like you to imagine for a moment the "ideal linguistic life" in terms of learning another language. Something you've never done before? Not surprising. Up until recently this would be considered the lofty idea of an Ivory Tower hermit. But today, with millions of families faced with the challenge of learning a foreign language, it is well worth considering and, as you will see soon, not only the stuff of dreams.

What if we could plan our child's whole linguistic life? If we could start from birth it is easy to imagine a "logical" course to pursue in order to achieve a high level of multilingualism. In the best of all worlds, the child's parents each speak their native language to their child (be they the same or different). The dominant language of the society (which may or may not be one of the parents' language) is "experienced" in daily life (trips to the park, supermarket excursions, and simply taking in the sights, smells, and sounds of the neighborhood). After the child ceases the normal mixing stage of his two languages—around three-and-a-half—he can then be considered orally bilingual. The child's increased socialization via contact with peers through daycare, playgroups, or formal schooling can introduce or reinforce a third language around this time if the parents wish. The child can learn pre-reading skills at home in one language before facing the same task at school (in the second or third language if the timing is right (which is explained later in *Multiliteracy Skills*). If the parents and school remain consistent in their strategies up to this point, the child should reach proficient oral levels in three languages and literacy (reading and writing) in two languages by around the time he is eight years old. Learning an additional language verbally could follow if desired at any time following this point. It is commonly suggested, though, that literacy skills in the third or fourth languages follow the proficient acquisition of the first then second language by a clear separation in timing.

What?! Be patient. Do not put this book down in disbelief. This utopian scenario may look unobtainable at first glance, but I have met a good number of families who have done exactly this and had the projected success with their languages and you, too, have the potential to do so as well. For example, a former student of mine was half-French, half-Japanese. Her parents each spoke their native language to her from birth, the mother in French and the father in Japanese. Before beginning school in Tokyo her mother taught her the French alphabet at home. At five years old she began attending the International School of the Sacred Heart in Tokyo in English. There she learned to read and write first in English and then later in Japanese. By the time I met her at age sixteen she spoke French, Japanese, and English with native or near-native fluency, and wrote in French and English perfectly, and Japanese with near-native fluency.

Another example has to do with a colleague and her children. From birth she spoke to them exclusively in Portuguese, her husband in Spanish. They attended an international school in Ecuador where they learned to read and write in Spanish and then English. Due to a family move, they finished schooling in Geneva, where they learned to speak, read, and write in French. By the time they graduated from high school they spoke Portuguese, Spanish, English, and French fluently. They could read and write in Spanish and English fluently, and in French with near-fluent ability.

TEN KEY FACTORS IN RAISING MULTILINGUAL CHILDREN

In these two cases, the families must have done something "terribly right," as the children had overwhelmingly positive experiences with their language learning and they not only became proficient bilinguals, but *multi-literate* in several languages. What were the key factors and why were they so successful in implementing them? Aside from each parent speaking a different language (that was different from the community language in one case and the same in the other), what other variables led to success? And what about your own family situation where the conditions for bilingualism are less "optimal" than those in the two cases presented above and where some factor does not fit the mold perfectly? In my research I have come across ten crucial factors that all have weight in successful multilingualism. As would be expected, each of the factors varies depending on the family, and each child puts them together differently, though all ten always play a role in each family's formula.

Of the ten key factors in raising multilingual children, seven have had a great deal written about them, and three have less "hard fact" supporting them, but they are included here for readers to evaluate according to their own family situations (See Figure 2.1). A bonus question would be to ask parents if they notice what is missing from this list. There is an extremely important, influential factor which impacts every child's approach to foreign language learning which is not noted. Do you know what it is?

If you realized that "Personality" is missing from this list, you win, and not only you personally, but probably your whole family because you see the importance of this factor. Personality is an influential component of whether or not a child is a successful polyglot. Personal characteristics can either compensate for or dilute one's abilities to learn any new activity. For example, an open, confident child may still achieve fluency in a language even if he has no aptitude, simply given the driving nature of his personality. A child with great aptitude can certainly become fluent, even if he is shy and slow to jump into the arena to try new things. Aptitude, opportunity, and personal characteristics all play a role, as does the physical structure of the brain. Why isn't Personality included in the list then? Because personalities can change. A child can stop being open and gregarious in school if always pushed into submission by a teacher unappreciative of that type of character. Or a child's self-esteem can be enhanced by a loving caregiver. Such situations are reflected in the Motivation and Opportunity categories. So while Personality is extremely important, it is not part of this recipe because the consequences of it are reflected in the other ingredients.

Back to the recipe.

Figure 2.1
Ten Key Factors in Raising Multilingual Children

1) Timing and The Windows of Opportunity

2) Aptitude for Foreign Languages

3) Motivation

4) Strategy

5) Consistency

6) Opportunity and Support: the Home Role,
    School Role, and the Community Role

7) The Linguistic Relationship between the First and
    Second Languages

8) Siblings

9) Gender

10) Hand Use

The last four of these ten factors cannot be changed. The linguistic relationship between your family's languages, how many siblings your child has at the moment, your child's gender, and his hand preference are all fixed variables. Why can't you influence these four? You cannot change your child's sex, force him to use his left hand if he is a "righty" (or visa versa), quickly add a baby sister into the picture to change the dynamics of the household, or force Chinese to be a Romance language. While these inalterable factors have to be considered and recognized for their influence—which we will do in chapter 8 when we evaluate our own families using the *Family Language Profile Worksheet*—the first six of the ten key factors *can* be manipulated and used to our advantage, and this leads us to our "recipe for success."

ONE RECIPE FOR SUCCESSFUL SECOND LANGUAGE ACQUISITION IN CHILDREN

1. **Windows of Opportunity**: Take advantage of the windows of opportunities for second language acquisition by either raising your child bilin-

gual from birth, or honing in on the times in early childhood where the brain is better equipped to receive new languages;

2. **Aptitude**: Take advantage of your child's aptitude for second language acquisition, or compensate for the lack thereof with numbers one, three, and four.

3. **Motivation**: Cultivate positive motivation and respect for the second language.

4. **Strategy** and

5. **Consistency**: Be consistent in the strategy you choose to use with your child and maintain a supportive home, school, and community environment.

6. **Opportunity**: Take advantage of the surroundings, the caregivers, and the school community as well as your and your spouse's languages to offer your child opportunities in language development.

The cook (parent) should be careful to measure the ingredients liberally. Too little motivation, for example, makes any amount of opportunity useless. Such is the case with a lack of consistency; your "cake" will not rise if it is missing. If there is no opportunity it is like an oven without heat, you'll never get the batter to form into a pastry. And if your child has aptitude and you do not recognize and capitalize on it, it is like forgetting to frost the cake, it could be just that much richer if you did! We begin with a summary of the ingredients and what parents have to do with them, then more about each one in detail.

Starting from the Beginning

Parents must determine which *Window of Opportunity* their child is in at present. Briefly, the First Window is from birth to nine months old. A Window-and-a-Half is from nine months through two and can be used by those children who are auditorily inclined (they have a "good ear"). The Second Window of Opportunity is from four to seven years old. The Third Window of Opportunity is from "Old Age and Back": it always exists and is categorized as from eight years old through adults. So if your son is eight, he is in the Third Window. If your daughter is five, she is in the Second Window. If your child is auditorily inclined and a year-and-a-half, he is in the Window-and-a-Half category. You and I are in the Third Widow. A newborn is in the First Window, and so on. The neurological basis for the theory of *Windows of Opportunity for Foreign Language Acquisition* is discussed in chapter 6. Once you as a parent have determined which Window your child is in you are able to decide which approaches will work best.

After determining the Window, the next step is to evaluate your child's *aptitude* for foreign languages, or his or her lack thereof. From there the role of *motivation*, both internal and external, positive and negative, must be considered. Parents must then agree upon a *strategy* to reach family language goals and be *consistent* in their approach. The child must have the *opportunity* to use his languages, and the support to pursue them from the home, his school, and the community. If all of this takes place, a Multilingual Child is born of your efforts.

A word now about each of these areas in depth. Chapter 3, *Ingredients*, goes into detail about the Windows of Opportunity and the role of Aptitude. Chapter 4, *Baking Instructions*, clarifies using the roles of Motivation, Strategy, and Consistency to your advantage. Chapter 5, *Kitchen Design*, identifies the type of language environment you are in and the Opportunity it gives you to cultivate foreign language. This chapter also looks at how your child's native language can influence your second language, depending on how they are related linguistically, and on the role of Siblings. Chapter 6, *Plumbing and Electricity*, focuses on the Multilingual Brain, the role of Gender on language learning, and how Hand Use may indicate a difference in language learning styles.

ᐁᕿᐁ

Chapter 3

Ingredients

GOURMET TIPS

Any chef will tell you that there are some things she just cannot cook without. For some it may be the basics of a certain brand of flour, for others it is the dash of salt that brings out the flavor. In the case of raising multilingual children, there are two essentials: the Window of Opportunity and the child's level of Aptitude for foreign language acquisition. These two factors are discussed separately from all the others as they are vital to every family's recipe, though they will invariably come in different measures for each. Carefully study the descriptions to determine what Window your child is in, then gauge her Aptitude for foreign language learning based on the explanation below.

TAKING ADVANTAGE OF THE WINDOWS OF OPPORTUNITY

Taking advantage of nature's own Windows of Opportunity can be your key ingredient, as all of the other important factors take place, or are developed, within the environs of the Window. This "base" element is like the flour in bread, so essential, yet so simple. The

Figure 3.1
Windows of Opportunity

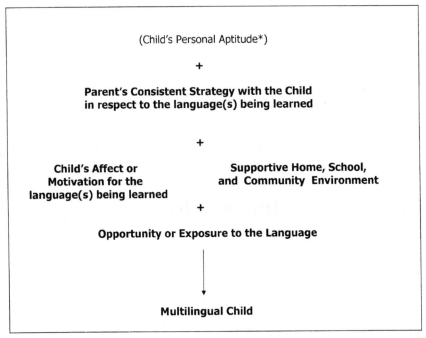

(Child's Personal Aptitude*)

+

**Parent's Consistent Strategy with the Child
in respect to the language(s) being learned**

+

**Child's Affect or   Supportive Home, School,
Motivation for the   and Community Environment
language(s) being learned**

+

Opportunity or Exposure to the Language

Multilingual Child

*May or may not contribute to the formula depending on whether the child has high
    aptitude or low aptitude.

Windows are the Timing with which a new language is introduced
to your child (see Figure 3.1)

The First Window of Opportunity is from birth to nine months
old. This Window is sometimes stretched to two years for those children who are auditorily inclined. During this time the best "medicine" is words. The more you talk to your child the better. The more
languages he can be exposed to the more chances he has of using this
information later to actually learn another language. At this point in
your child's life languages are "acquired" rather than "learned"; they
are part and parcel of his developing being; languages are "naturally"
incorporated into a child's repertoire of abilities. When a child is
exposed to a language, any language, at this time, he is making connections in his brain which can be *retraced* later in life to actually
speak that language. This is in stark contrast to a child who has not
had any exposure to other languages and who makes his first connec-

tions in the brain *while* he learns to speak (the Second Window). Or the adult, who makes the first connections while learning to speak *and* write simultaneously (in the Third Window). We adults must learn a language as opposed to the infant's acquisition of it (Richards and Rodgers 1986). So even though you may not be able to see (or hear) the pay-off of such exposure (very few zero- to nine-month-olds speak well enough to tell you), you can be sure your child is absorbing the sounds around him and this will serve him later in life. While recorded songs, rhymes, and videos may not hurt your child, nothing replaces an actual human being when it comes to the delivery of language. Basically, at this age, the more human contact and verbal exchange your child can have with parents, siblings, and caregivers, the better.

The Second Window of Opportunity is from four to seven years old. This is the best time to introduce a child to a second language if he was raised monolingual from birth, and this is a perfect time to offer an already bilingual child a third language. This is a very special time in a child's life for two influential reasons related to language development. First, children this age are still open to the idea of using language as a game. They have very small or non-existent egos to block their attempts at speaking. When they are corrected, they take it as a new rule to the game and not as a personal attack. The idea of speaking a new language is much like a code to small children, and with this idea come intrigue and renewed attempts to master the mystery of the rules. Second, children this age are usually in school, and with school comes the opportunity for exposure to and use of other languages. For the child who has been brought abroad in a temporary move by his parents, say from the United States to Germany, or from Poland to Spain, language is the vehicle through which he can establish himself. By speaking the language he "earns" friends, well worth the price of the initial bumbled sentences and small vocabulary. For the newly arrived immigrant child, say from Thailand to Canada, the new language means survival on every level.

At the beginning of the Second Window the discussion is mainly related to verbal language skills. While there are linguistically correct ways to define "bilingual," which we will address in chapter 8, for now let it suffice to say that when we identify a "bilingual four-year-old" we mean that the child speaks two languages. This is a time of opportunity for families who have biliteracy skills (reading and writing in two languages) as the long-term goal for their children. This makes the introduction of the written word in a child's native language at home imperative at this point if biliteracy skills are part of the family's language goals (see chapter 8). In general, this means teaching letters and their phonic sounds in the child's native language at home before they do so in the second language at school. Depending on the school system in which the child finds himself, this can occur at age four, five, six, or even seven (some Scandinavian countries do not begin teaching reading until eight years old, for example). For a better list of when different countries begin teaching writing, see *Multiliteracy Skills* in chapter 8.

The Third Window of Opportunity is always present and is generally associated with anyone who has not learned a second language in infancy or early childhood. This Window is opened at eight years of age and never shuts. While children have the edge over adults in one way when it comes to learning languages, adults have advantages in other mental realms. As shown by numerous studies, humans never lose the capacity to learn a foreign language. Adolescent and adult learners are actually better than small children in grasping abstract concepts of syntax and grammar. If the child (eight years and older) is to learn a new language in the Third Window, presumably after having learned to read and write in his native language, then parents need to understand that this is a very different mental process from the child who has learned his languages simultaneously from birth. Parents with children in the Third Window must show support at home and request backing from the school in reinforcing second language acquisition. On a positive note, parents and older children learning another language at this point should take heart at the studies that prove that those who devote time to language learning are bound to have as much success as the younger children around them.

Identifying the Window is like understanding whether whole wheat flour works better than pastry flour in your particular family recipe. Depending on which Window your child is in, read the following descriptions in depth to better sympathize with what special challenges emerge from this moment in his life.

The First Window of Opportunity (Zero to Nine Months)

If your child is in the First Window, count yourself lucky. It seems that children are born "universal listeners" (Werker 1997) or receivers of language sounds. They can distinguish between foreign languages' fine phonemes and extremely subtle sounds (the English "p" and "b" for example) from the very first days of life. I read a study once, retold in a magazine (Cowley 1997: 17), that illustrated how four-day-old infants showed a preference for their native language, be it French or Russian. In this simple test, it was shown that Russian babies sucked harder when hearing Russian than they did when hearing French. French babies did just the opposite and sucked harder when they heard French than when they heard Russian. In a series of more complex studies of young infants, grouped from six to eight months old, eight to ten months old, and ten to twelve months old, illustrated their ability to recognize sounds that adults were not able to distinguish (Werker 1997). Werker and Tees (1984a) found that languages as different as Zulu, Hindi, Spanish and Czech—which have sounds which are unrecognizable to adult English speakers—posed no problem for English-speaking infants. This was clearly seen by watching a machine which measured the electrical firing of synapses in different areas of the brain when different sounds were heard. The researchers also found an interesting learning curve; children differed greatly in their abilities depending on their age. The youngest performed the best. Nearly all the six to eight month-old infants scored in the highest range on auditory ability to differentiate sounds. The eight to ten-month-olds had mixed scores and the ten to twelve-month-olds scored the lowest. Werker repeated this study at two month intervals and found that *as the children got older, they lost their ability to be "universal listeners."* Tsushima et al. (1994) conducted a similar study with Japanese infants and found that the younger set (six to eight-month-olds) could distinguish the English *ra* vs. *la*, but the older infants could not. Patricia Kuhl et al. (1992) of the University of Washington has done similar studies that duplicate these findings, and most recently, K. Kim and Joy Hirsch (1997) have confirmed these findings. This would explain why some cognitive scientists are putting a threshold of seven to nine months old on children learning more than one language fluently.

In April 1997 I heard a very intriguing interview with neurologist Dr. A. Diamond who believes that up to the age of seven months all languages are received in the same place in the brain as the "first" language. This means that a child can take in several languages early in life and treat them all as "first" languages, as seen in multilingual societies such as Malaysia (where Chinese, Malay, and English can be found together). This contention is supported by two classics in the field of linguistics. Both Werner Leopold's records (1939–1949) of his English-German bilingual daughter and Jules Ronjat's book (1913) on his French-German bilingual son, indicate that infant bilinguals—those who learn two languages simultaneously from birth—initially treat their language systems as a single unit, and later "separate" or distinguish them as two different language systems sometime between two-and-a-half and three-and-a-half years old. So instead of learning "Greek" and "Turkish," the child perceives them as just one language. Other informal records by parents of multilinguals, which we will see at the end of this section, lend weight to the idea that children receive multiple languages as a single unit if taught from birth. After nine months, however, there is a change in how the brain receives foreign languages. This change occurs because of the increased connections between cells which are now formed due to the child's rapid growth and to his experiences in the world.

Touch just above your left ear and above your left eyebrow. Basically, if you are right-handed, left-hemisphere dominant, your primary language area is here, in the left parietal and left frontal lobes. Neuroscientists have observed for almost a hundred years that in the rare cases where children suffer strokes in the language area of their brains, they often recover language skills, using the right hemisphere as a type of "back-up" system (Mai et al. 1998; Restak 1984). New research seems to indicate that languages introduced after nine months old would tend to utilize more of the *right* hemisphere than regular language location in a monolingual.

Going back to our First Window: Sometime between seven and nine months old, say present-day neurologists, enough neuroconnections are formed to separate the location of first and second languages in the brain. While this idea was observed in a somewhat different form by Leopold and Ronjat sixty and eighty-five years earlier, respectively, the use of modern equipment to actually measure brain activity did not come about until the late seventies when a study was conducted by Fred Genesee (1979) and his colleagues classifying "early" and "late" bilinguals. They measured bilingual subjects' brain activity on an electroencephalograph (EEG) while they named in which language different words were being presented to them. Fascinatingly enough, they found that those who were bilingual from birth showed greater use of their left hemispheres, which is where one's first language is usually located. In contrast, those who learned their languages after early childhood showed greater use of their *right* hemispheres. This confirms that multiple languages learned at birth are all treated as the "first" language.

Between seven and nine months of age cells in the brain that were once receptive to "foreign" sounds begin to atrophy and die off if not used, or perhaps a better word here is "rehearsed." This explains why the older infants (ten to twelve months) in Werker's tests scored lowest. Since the infants had no exposure to the language sounds except when being tested, they presumably did not "rehearse" these neuro-connections and thus, they failed to thrive. While not a part of Werker's tests, it can be assumed by other case studies that those people who had continued exposure to the language sounds—that is, they heard the foreign language with some regularity either through friends, neighbors, caregivers, or teachers—forged enough synaptic connections in the area to retain the language and speak it later in life. This is a key point.

Passive Language Acquisition

The assumption here is that if, as an infant or small child, you have regular exposure to a language, you are "learning it" on a subconscious level. Though your infant son may not appear to be taking in the neighbor's constant chatter, television noises, and the children in the yard playing in Spanish, he is actually developing a type of "passive bilingualism." This passive bilingualism can move into the realm of active, or functional, bilingualism later in life with formal study and practice. In effect, he is "rehearsing" the connections between neurons vital to the life of that language by being exposed to it.

To carry the point further that consistent exposure to the language is necessary to maintain the ability to differentiate subtle sounds not found in your native language, it was shown in Werker's tests that adults who were given the same sets of language sounds to hear scored even *lower* than the twelve-month-olds. This lends weight to the idea that "adults just don't seem to pick up languages like children." This is true, adults do not learn in the *same* way. However, while adults and children differ in the way languages are stored in the brain, the results can be equally positive. As many of us who have tried to learn a foreign language in adulthood can confirm, adults *do* have the ability to compensate for this natural, albeit youthful, ability to hear and reproduce sounds. While adults may be handicapped by the inability to form fresh neuro-connections and distinguish sounds effortlessly, they are able to *consciously* decide to learn the sounds, and with time, to reproduce them. In other words, adults can be taught (or train themselves) to do what comes naturally to children.

Accents

While adults may flawlessly learn the grammar and syntax of a language, few adult second language learners reach a point of proficiency where they are able to speak a language without an accent. This may be in part due to the lack of neuro-connections in the speech area of the brain, it may be due to the lack of application, or in many cases, there is a physical limitation in the ability of one's mouth to form phonemes for which it has never practiced. For example, while a great many Japanese know English grammar as well as or better than the average American, most have a very hard time differentiating the English *ra* and *la* or the difference between *fu* and *hu* because there is no distinction in Japanese. Similarly, many people who learn English later in life have extreme difficulty with the English "th" which is a consonant combination not found in many other languages. Those adults who can speak a foreign language without an accent, however, are addressed in the following "Window and a Half" group.

The First Window of Opportunity can be defined as from birth to nine months of age, but in some very special cases, this can be extended for those who are auditorily inclined, as we shall see in the special group that follows.

A Window and a Half (Up to Two Years Old)

An "extension" of this First Window exists in some children who have particularly good auditory perception. Just as some of us are born with the potential to be great artists or mathematicians or dancers or painters, some people are born with great auditory memory and listening abilities. These are the people we say have "a good ear." Such children can take advantage of the fact that the auditory cortex of the brain never completely rules out the ability to receive and interpret sounds from other languages, though it does narrow drastically sometime around two years of age. Simple exposure to a foreign language through music tapes, conversations with caregivers, or visits to relatives in foreign countries (or the neighbor's constant chatter mentioned earlier) can contribute to a person's ability to learn a language later in life. In other words, if an auditorily inclined child has not learned a second language before two years old but has had exposure to the language, he will then be able to draw on this experience when he is older to learn to speak the second language with more ease than a person who is not so auditorily inclined. This goes back to the statement in the previous section with regard to "passive bilinguals." Whereas the child may not appear to be absorbing any part of the language, she is, in fact, reinforcing and rehearsing neuro-connections related to a new language. I firmly believe that having been raised for the first years of my life in east Los Angeles with Spanish-speaking neighbors aided greatly in my ability to learn Spanish as a high school student with no strong accent (or so says my Ecuadorian husband). Simple exposure (verbal exchanges, playing, cooking, sharing meals, etc.) to these early Mexican friends planted some strong foundations and neuro-connections in the speech area and auditory cortex of my brain giving me pathways to *retrace* in adolescence as opposed to building from scratch. We can define the First Window, then, as being from zero to nine months, and extending to two years old in some cases where the person is auditorily inclined.

Outside the Windows, But Still in the Ball Park: Something Special at Three-and-a-Half-Years-Old

There is a point, however, between the ages of approximately two and four years old where the learning curve for foreign languages seems to stagnate. Ask the pre-school teachers around you. They all agree that three-year-olds seem hard-pressed to learn a language, but "give them another year, it will come" is often advised with a knowing smile.

Children may continue to perfect what languages they have been exposed to earlier in life, and many learn something about an entirely new language passively, but oral fluency in the new tongue will be put off until about the age of four. The explanation? One guess is that at just before twelve months old most children utter their first words. By the time they hit eighteen months there is an explosion of new vocabulary, and by the time the child is two she is often speaking in complete (although short and grammatically incorrect) sentences (e.g., "mommy juice more!"), perhaps not allowing for the "distraction" of another language at this time. Zero to three years old is the time of greatest cognitive growth in a human's lifetime and here the solidification in one's first-language skills occurs, perhaps explaining why there is little room for a new language until the following year.

Something very special happens between two-and-a-half and three-and-a-half years old, however. At this age children are able to distinguish and label languages. By three-and-a-half almost every child knows the name of the language(s) he speaks, and can tell which people share his tongue(s). "Mommy speaks Spanish and Daddy speaks Italian," or "I speak English and Grandma speaks Japanese" are typical examples of labeling. This conscious naming of languages is a huge cognitive leap from simple utilization. This is a clear milestone between children who learn languages in the First Window and those who do so in the Second Window. There is a very special time right around three-and-a-half to four years old when many children appear to "blossom" in their language abilities. Perhaps this is because they grow beyond their initial "mixing" stage to this conscious separation of languages. Many parents of bilingual children complain of their child's "slowness to speak," only to find that, happily, at about four years old there is no distinction between their child and the average monolingual. This solidification of skills is a welcome relief to the confused sentences of the first years. Actually learning a new language (second or third) does not seem to occur between two and four years old. This is made up for, however, in the Second Window of Opportunity, as we will see next.

The Second Window of Opportunity (Four to Seven Years Old)

A Second Window of Opportunity emerges between the ages of four and seven years old. Why does this occur? Perhaps because children now have a firm base in whatever language(s) they have been surrounded with in the first year or two of life, and the fine tuning of more "sophisticated" neuro-connections into a second language learning area of the brain can be formed (Bialystock and Hakuta 1995). For children who were already early or simultaneous bilinguals, at about three-and-a-half years old, they generally cease to mix languages and can identify which language goes with which person, giving way to the possibility of a third or fourth language at this time.

Or equally feasible is an explanation founded in psychology as opposed to neurology or linguistics.

Generally speaking, children under the age of seven (unless extremely shy to begin with) are not inhibited by making mistakes in public. Language is a game, a code, to be played with. When children make a mistake in pronunciation or do not know the right word in a situation, they ask, or make it up, or use something close to what they need. If and when they are corrected they accept it as part of the rules to the game and move on; no ego-bruising, no blushing or hiding or closing their mouths for the rest of the afternoon just because someone had to help them. At this young age, children's egos do not get in the way of speaking (or many other areas of their lives, as a matter of fact). I remember at the end of the first day of kindergarten for my daughter, Natalie, she was saying goodbye to a new friend. "*Tschüss Isabél!*" she yelled enthusiastically in German. She said *Isabel* with a bit of a Spanish ring to it, instead of the German that the little girl was, and so Isabel laughed, "*Tschüss Isabél!*" she mimicked. And they both laughed. I would have curled up into a little ball and slid out of the room so that no one would notice what a disaster I had made out of the German "s" sound (more like an English "z") and the Spanish "s" sound. Instead, Natalie laughed at herself, and repeated her goodbye with the correction ("*Izábel*"), then left, waving happily.

Unfortunately, this honeymoon with the world's stage lasts just another few short years. Somewhere between six and seven years old little ones start, sadly enough, to become self-conscious. They start to care about what others think of them. They worry about what others say about them, how they speak, act, and dress. They start to act in ways to either avoid embarrassment or to gain recognition. I remember watching my daughter at her first ballet lesson. She was five years-two months at the time and was having a ball. She loved the fantasy of the wall-to-wall mirrors and the beautiful pictures of the dancers in flowing costumes and tutus. She listened eagerly to every word the instructor uttered, although it was her first introduction to French. She followed the examples with gusto and a kind of childish glee. She attended this first class with a good friend, who was seven and spoke French. This little girl entered the room cautiously, covering her leotard-covered chest as if in embarrassment, and continually pulled down the tights over her backside. She hesitated starting a move, and strove to keep count with the teacher and guarded her every step. What a difference two years can make!

Leaving the Childhood Windows: The Magic of Eight Years Old

We are born with more brain cells than we will ever use. And where no connections are formed, cells die off. Eight years old is a key time in a child's brain development. A child's life experiences up to age seven form her treasure chest of neuro-connections. What she has been lucky enough to hear, smell, taste, touch, and see up to this point are the basis for all future learning. As mentioned earlier, a child who suffers a stroke up to the age of six or seven years old often experiences no negative effect on language development (Geschwind 1997; Restak 1984). This illustrates the brain's plasticity up to this point, which allows for the "relocation" of skills if their "home" is damaged. Gleitman and Newport (1995) identify that the major spurts in brain development that are related to language production level off at age seven. The huge number of neurons we are born with begin to die off, first a large number at birth, then over the next seven years. Then the creation of new synapses "bottoms out," according to linguist Steven Pinker, around puberty, which could explain that such milestones in brain development parallel our ability to learn languages over the life span. "The language learning circuitry of the brain is more plastic in childhood; children learn or recover language when the left hemisphere of the brain is damaged or even surgically removed, but comparable damage in an adult usually leads to permanent aphasia [loss of language]," writes Pinker (1995).

While the Second Window "shuts" at age seven, there is something very special about eight years old. It is at this time, approximately the middle of second or third grade, when the playing field is leveled once again. That is, children who learned to read at seven-and-a-half and those who did so at three years old are just about even in their abilities. Boys who may have started out quieter than their female counterparts catch up and often surpass them in terms of verbal expression and general loudness. And whereas first-borns may have been faster at obtaining some skills up to this point (rolling over earlier, sitting earlier, walking earlier, talking earlier), at age eight it is impossible to tell children's birth order by observing their skills. This cognitive consolidation marks the difference in development between the infant and the nearly completely formed eight-year-old brain.

Eight-Year-Olds, Adolescents, and Adults: Same Size Brain, Same Way of Learning?

Of course not. Eight-year-olds are much different when it comes to learning a language from their teenage counterparts who are in turn different from full-grown adults, although they do have roughly the same size brain. At birth the human brain is approximately 350 grams. At one month it is about 420 grams; at one year it is 1,400 grams; eight years old about 2,800, the same as an adult's (Restak 1984). So while the brain of eight-year-olds, adolescents, and adults weigh nearly the same, any parent can tell you that it is a different experience, indeed, getting an eight-year-old to learn a new language, than it is for a teenager, or learning one themselves. Why is this?

Perhaps Judith Rich Harris offers us the answer in her *group socialization theory*, explained in her controversial book *The Nurture Assumption* (1998). An eight-year-old learns a new language differently from his adolescent sister because he has different peers, or in Harris' terms, a different group. If those peers are speaking a different language and he yearns to be a part of the group, he too will learn the language. If his adolescent sister, on the other hand, belongs to a different group (as she most certainly will, being older and a female), she may or may not find the same urge to learn the new language. If she joins the group that disdains the new language, she will not have any motivation to learn it. This is the same reason why bilingual education in the United States has failed, argues Harris. As a teenager at Berkeley High School, I remember watching some students spend four years in the "ESL track," meaning they started off being labeled non-English-language speakers, and maintained that identity throughout high school. These students were able to find a group and flourish as a result of their inability to speak English, not despite it. In fact, if they did eventually learn the new language they would be kicked out of their original group (the "ESL track") and have to begin searching for their group status all over again. This made learning English something to be avoided rather than coveted.

This enlightening argument also gives weight to teaching foreign languages to younger students as well. If we value our children knowing a second language, why do we begin instruction in Spanish, French, or German (or other languages if the school has the resources to do so) so late in a child's life? Most high schools in the United States have a foreign language requirement, most junior high schools do not, and it is very rare to find a middle school or elementary school which even offers a foreign language program. Wouldn't our resources be better spent targeting a receptive audience rather than a resistant one? Teaching six-year-olds songs, games, counting, animals, and colors in French would be a much more rewarding endeavor than shoveling points of grammar at a seventeen-year-old with hopes of enough retention that he can score well on the American Advance Placement exam. The key, according to Harris, would be to treat the whole group to the experience, not just separating out a few, who would then be ostracized from their peers. If the whole group, all of the first-graders, let's say, were treated to a few hours of French (or Spanish or Russian or Thai) each week, not only would their scores on those AP exams be higher when they finally got to taking them, but the entire experience with the foreign language would be improved. And since the respect for different languages would be enhanced by such early learning, the status afforded those students who already knew a different language (those in the "ESL track") would be higher and "bilingual" would stop being a negative label in the schools, and grow into an enviable one.

The Second Window of Opportunity is a special time precisely because it covers a time in a child's life which is generally spent in school (four to seven years old). Many children learn their second languages within a group setting in school. School policy, however, is beyond the scope of this book (see August and Hakuta, 1998, for more on this topic), and so we leave this intriguing area for the time being and move on to the Third Window.

The Third Window (From Old Age and Back)

The Third Window of Opportunity in language development is one that has to be built as it is not incorporated into our "mental house" as a given. How do we know there is such a thing? If no such window existed, then no seventh-grader in our public school system would ever reach competency levels in a foreign language, and no adult in the foreign service would ever be "trainable" in another tongue. The Third Window is purposefully vast. It literally covers age eight through old age, though we pointed out in the preceding section that there are differences in the way an eight-year-old, an adolescent, and an adult learn their languages. These differences are founded primarily in sociological and psychological factors, however, as neurologically the mechanics are the same. Pre-adolescents, teen-agers, and their parents have varying degrees of success not because of when they learn their languages (they are all in the Third Window), but due to the influence of the other "ingredients": Why (Motivation), how (Aptitude), and under what circumstances (Opportunity and Support) they do so.

As mentioned earlier, adults can be taught to discriminate sounds and can practice and train themselves in pronunciation. Adult learners can in fact "learn to discriminate between different sounds faster and better than children, as well as producing them more accurately," insist Harding and Riley (1996:63) if and when they are able to devote the same amount of time as children do when learning the second language. Birgit Harley (1986:14) writes that "because of greater cognitive maturity . . . older learners may have the ability to learn at least some aspects of a [second language] more efficiently than younger learners." Adults have the edge on studying languages when it comes to consciously learning grammatical structures and other rules because they understand the labels and are used to searching for patterns in speech. Children have the edge when it comes to leaping in and experimenting with a language.

Candyland, Monopoly, and Other Childhood Follies

I guess you could say that this is very similar to board games. When my husband and my daughter pull out a new board game (Candyland, Chutes and Ladders, Monopoly, etc.), my husband will carefully and methodically read every rule before doing anything else. My daughter will open the packages of cards and playing pieces and, if my husband takes too long, will make up her own game according to the materials she has to work with. A collaborator and mother of multilingual children, Cherise Valles McGivern, calls this the difference between knowing a language "cerebrally" versus "intuitively." Parents "think" a language, young children "sense" it. This is a tangible difference between adult and child foreign language learners which we grown-ups wrestle with in research (Shrum and Glisan 1999) since we cannot benefit from kids writing up similar studies.

The Third Window of Opportunity plays on our "mental maturity" to help us learn languages beyond early childhood. The brain has the fascinating ability to learn throughout the life span, though connections may have to be forged as opposed to coming automatically as happens in infancy. I was extremely intrigued at the visit of a stroke victim to our neuropsychology class at the Harvard Extension school in 1997. The subject was a fifty-one-year-old man who had been a professor at MIT in Physics. His stroke was so severe that they had to remove a quarter to a third of his brain (left posterior and parietal lobes) in emergency surgery, and the doctor assumed he would be extremely handicapped once he recovered from his physical wounds. When he spoke to us, he broke many of the known rules about the brain's ability to learn or compensate for losses later in life which I would like to share here.

It has been known for over a hundred years that brain cells can never regenerate: there is no such thing as a new brain cell. You actually have fewer brain cells than you were born with, as those that were not "employed" in youth have now atrophied. Your ability to learn is based on how many cells you have and what connections you make between them. While the brain's plasticity in childhood is well noted and is in fact the basis for all new learning, it is also known that brain cells begin to die off from the minute we are born. In this stroke victim's case, his learning feat was extraordinary for two reasons. First, as an older man it would be expected that new learning would come as a difficulty. Second, he had much less of his brain to work with. He tells how initially he had trouble recognizing faces, could only remember his own name and that of his dog, and had no knowledge of the Physics which had been his life's work up until that early summer morning when he collapsed in his garden. His ability to read had been impaired to the extent that "sight recognition" of words was gone, and he had to sound out every letter in order to be able to read. But, with the help of a therapist and the undying devotion (and insistence) of his wife, he learned to speak again, though a good part of the brain associated with language had been completely removed. This means that a different part of the brain had taken over the job of the verbal cortex; a kind of "forced transfer" had occurred, and new synapses had been made in order to allow him to speak again. This extraordinary man "built" a Third Window of Opportunity for his *native* language. I have since reflected that if he could do that with just three-fourths of his brain, I suppose that each of us as adults could do so with a whole one!

Another intriguing fact that supports the existence of a Third Window of Opportunity is that there are people on record who are capable of speaking fifty-eight languages or more (*Guinness Book of World Records 1999*). In each case, multiple languages were not all learned simultaneously from birth, rather they were accumulated over the individual's life span, meaning new languages were learned in the First Window, the Second Window, and "from old age and back," the Third Window. Other cases, like a good friend's uncle, boast the ability to read and write fluently in fourteen languages, though this man "only" spoke competently in three or four. It seems he learned Spanish while in school in Colombia, then while attending the French school there he learned German as a "second" language. He later took up English, Russian, Arabic, Hebrew, Greek, and Latin, to name a few. All this learning took place in the Third Window. And then there is the popular story about Berlitz, the father of the Berlitz Language School, who learned four or five languages simultaneously as a child. It seems he had different caregivers who each spoke to him in a different language, so by school age he already was fluent in multiple languages. He went on to study even more in school and in adulthood knew some twelve languages. These stories, while not your typical cases, do give us comfort related to knowing that languages can be learned throughout the life span by constructing the panes of this Third Window of Opportunity.

SOME SUCCESSFUL RECIPES USING THE WINDOWS

Now for some illustration of the Windows. These descriptions should serve the same purpose as photos of a finished meal in cookbooks often do; to give the cook an idea of what can be expected. All cases are referred to in Appendix B.

Ana: A German Spaniard or a Spanish German?

Ana (case VVVV) is a special case of a woman whose parents are Spanish but who was brought up in Germany. She learned Spanish at home, but insists that her first language is German due to the strong influence of her surroundings, the family maid, and her schooling. She learned to read and write first in German, and later did so in Spanish. Ana is a polyglot (German, Spanish, English, and some French), and her husband's native language is Spanish and he knows some English, French, and German, which he has acquired through formal study in each language. Ana is a professor of German language in a Spanish university. The family has two children: a four-year-old daughter and a one-year-old son, and they currently live in France near the Swiss border. She speaks to her children exclusively in German, and her husband speaks to them in Spanish. The daughter attends the German School, and so her stronger language is now German. The mother feels that she wants her children to know German, though their roots are Spanish, because "it's a gift I can give to them." The younger daughter is four years old, and has yet to cease mixing her languages, though this does not concern her mother, who says nonchalantly, "Just think how long it takes to learn one language well. I can wait twice that long to have her speak two."

Ana learned both Spanish and German in the First Window and speaks both fluently. Her daughter was exposed to both German and Spanish from birth, and has heard both parents speaking in Spanish and knows her father also understands a lot of German. Her mother was her only source of German until she began attending the German School at age three. German and Spanish are not similar languages, German having Germanic roots and Spanish, Latin roots. While Ana has tried to be consistent in strategy, her husband tends to mix Spanish and German. Both parents are currently learning French. I am guessing Ana's daughter's language skills will come into full force in the Second Window, which she has just entered, hopefully by first ceasing to mix, then by increasing her fluidity and vocabulary in both German and Spanish.

Let's go back to the recipe metaphor. Each successful recipe of a multilingual includes the Windows of Opportunity, Aptitude, Motivation, Strategy, Consistency, and the Opportunity to use the languages. While each ingredient has a role to play, in Ana's case, the fact that she was exposed to her languages when she was an infant facilitated her learning tremendously and is thus the most important ingredient in her mix. She obviously has a high aptitude for languages and was given the opportunity to use them daily, also facilitating her learning.

The Swiss Woman and the Italian Man Who Brought Up Their Children in German

Another family is composed of a Swiss-Italian couple (case D) who speak French at home. The parents are both polyglots (father: Italian, German, French, and English; mother: French, English, some Italian, and learning German). The father's parents speak German, though he himself was raised in Italy. Their two boys hear Italian on vacations and the older speaks French and German fluently, though his German vocabulary needs improvement. He also has a passive knowledge of Italian. The younger child speaks primarily in French, though it is clear he understands what is said in German. The older child is learning to read in French now before he will have to do so in German next year. The mother believes her children are "average" in terms of aptitude. She spends a great deal of time with her children reading at home in French. The family's goals are to have the children speak enough German, French, and Italian to communicate with their relatives, and that they learn to read and write well in French before doing so in German next year.

The two right-handed boys learned their native French in the First Window and had exposure to Italian and German in the same. They learned German more formally in the Second Window through schooling. The opportunity to hear and practice Italian and German on vacations has been valuable in these children's language development as their parents have always spoken exclusively in French to avoid any confusion. The similarity between Italian and French (both Romance languages with Latin roots) may have helped their learning.

The older boy's recipe relies greatly on his having been introduced to his languages at birth (taking advantage of the Windows of Opportunity), and the parents' consistent strategy (one-person, one-language) which has facilitated his learning. Visiting German-speaking and Italian-speaking relatives has provided a highly motivational opportunity for the boy as well.

What Do You Get When a Greek Polyglot Marries an Ecuadorian–American Polyglot? (A "Glottal Stop" . . . Linguistic Humor)

Juan's parents are American and Ecuadorian (case BBBB), and he is a polyglot (Spanish, English, German, and French). He fell in love with and married a Greek (case CCCC) who was born in the United States. Maria is also a polyglot (English, Greek, some Spanish, and learning French). They have recently moved to Paris where he is working as a lawyer and she is studying for another Master's degree. When discussing the possibility of having children, their situation is a delightful fountainhead of possibilities. Juan learned English from his mother and Spanish from his father, German in school, and French while in the university. He later went on to study his law degree in Paris, attesting to his high level of French. Maria learned Greek at home and English from her environment in the United States. The family then returned to Greece where she finished her studies. She studied Spanish and later worked for the World Bank on projects in Latin America, attesting to her level of proficiency in the language. She is currently studying French. They acknowledge that they have a "knack" for languages and find them "fun" to learn as opposed to requiring effort. They also recognize their importance in terms of getting a job in today's world. "When we were deciding where to live after we married we pulled out a map and marked all of the countries with all of the languages we could work in," says Maria excitedly. They chose Paris despite Maria's lack of French because she was sure it would just "be a matter of time." The couple is now considering children and have a wonderful problem: in which of their many languages should they speak to their child? One scenario would be that Maria speak in Greek, Juan in English, and let the French come from the environment. As Spanish is close to French (both Romance languages), they reason, he or she will "get it" with exposure to the paternal family side over vacations. Another scenario is that Maria speak in English, Juan in Spanish, the French comes from the environment, and that he or she learns Greek on visits to the maternal side of the family. In any case, they "expect" that their child should have at least three languages before he/she enters grade school. Not bad for a glottal stop!

Juan and Maria are exceptional cases where all ingredients have played a nearly equal part in their multilingualism, though their exceptional aptitude and the introduction of their first languages early in life proved pivotal.

Now we go from the all-encompassing Windows of Opportunity to the specific elements inside. The first factor has to do with aptitude for foreign languages, something your child may or may not have. How can you determine if your child has an aptitude for foreign languages, and what can we do with that information when we have it? This is what we turn to next.

YOUR CHILD'S APTITUDE FOR FOREIGN LANGUAGES

I have a friend who believes that all success in language depends on individual aptitude. Some people are born able to speak languages, while others just do not have such gifts. Needless to say, she has a high aptitude for languages, as do her children, so her hypothesis fits her needs. But aptitude, like all of our other ingredients, cannot be viewed in isolation. Even if a child has a very high aptitude for foreign languages, if he lives in the middle of a corn field in Iowa and never has the chance to use it, it is useless. If a child has plenty of aptitude but no motivation, it is doubtful he will ever reach a true proficiency level in his languages. And a third scenario is also true: a child with very low aptitude for languages can still become a proficient bilingual if he has been exposed to multiple languages since infancy and is given many opportunities and strong encouragement from his home, school, and community environments.

Just as you and I have a different aptitude in music, we also have a different aptitude for language learning. Your daughter has a certain aptitude for math which is different from your son's aptitude in baseball. Your niece has a different aptitude for "coloring between the lines" which is different from your nephew's aptitude for tightrope walking. Different people have varying abilities when it comes to speaking foreign languages. While you have given your child all the aptitude she will get in her life through your genes, you can at the present no more influence her aptitude in language learning than you can the color of her eyes. (There has been no proof of a gene responsible for language aptitude, but with current gene mapping it is only a matter of time. In a very high percentage of cases presented here, for example, multilingual children have polyglot parents. While this could also be attributed to the type of life multilinguals lead, the argument for a biological base for the high correlation is great.) You *can* compensate for any deficiency in aptitude, however, with a motivating home environment and by offering your child opportunities for language cultivation. By offering encouragement for your child's attempts at a foreign language, you can boost his affinity for it, and this helps tremendously. But what if you are unsure if your child does or does not have aptitude for foreign languages?

There are certain signs to be conscious of when observing small children and evaluating their language abilities. By giving your child the chance to experience as many different kinds of stimuli as possible, you can observe her reactions and gauge which she seems attracted to, or is better at. For example, when you repeatedly offer your daughter the choice to either watercolor, play with a puzzle, or dance to a noisy instrument you can begin to recognize her talents (or lack thereof) in these areas. Such activities measure creativity, fine motor control, logical manipulation of forms, and musical inclination. By exposing her to languages and word games early in life you can also get an idea of her interest and ability (or lack of) in language. Even very small children can be observed for their language inclination. A child with a "good ear" will have a fine sense of the "rhythm" of a conversation much earlier than she will have the words for the conversation itself. Many times she will babble, but you know exactly when she is forming a question by the rise in her voice at the end of her "sentence." She will exhibit a good memory for musical tunes, rhymes, and other word-related games. On the other hand, if you realize that your child is particularly poor in these areas, you can begin early to enhance what ability does exist. Practice will reinforce whatever aptitude (high or low) your child is born with.

While aptitude is something your child is born with, what he does with it depends on you, which is why it is considered in our recipe. Your child relies on you for starting on the right path. Who knows, had Beethoven never got his hands on a piano, who would have been the wiser? But thank goodness he did! Giving your child the chance to experience a variety of stimuli is the only way of knowing what he will be good at. This exposure to stimuli does not mean spending handfuls of money to get the latest toy, however. Does your child enjoy banging on pots and pans or hate the ruckus? Does she get a kick out of watching how the water goes down the drain or the intricacies of how an old wet leaf looks like it has a skeleton? Does he adore books or scribbling on paper, pretending to write to Grandma? Does she have a way with animals or a passion for plants? Whatever the particular talent, you need to make the most of what cognitive inclinations your child may have. In the realm of language development and second language acquisition, children's aptitude should be measured and taken into account. But do not be discouraged if you feel your child "simply hasn't got it," his talents are bound to lie elsewhere. By recognizing that he is not so strong in foreign languages when he is still young, you can help by focusing your energy on the other factors involved in language acquisition that you can directly influence to compensate for this dearth—the Windows of Opportunity and the timing of new language introduction, your consistent strategy, the school and community backing, and especially by giving your child opportunities to be exposed to and develop a love of language, even if he is not "good" at it.

Here is another tasty suggestion. Many a child has been attracted to tacos before he learned Spanish, to pizza before he heard Italian, chow mein before he knew about Chinese. Use other venues, such as food, to bring a language to life in your home and to measure foreign language aptitude. Some children love to play with foreign language sounds, but may not have many chances to do so. Using restaurant outings, or "foreign food nights" at home can give you the chance to observe your child's interaction with the language, albeit with limited, but delicious vocabulary.

The Research on Foreign Language Aptitude

Psychologist John Carroll and his colleague S. M. Sapon devised the Modern Foreign Language Aptitude Test (MFLAT) in 1958 to predict the performance of students in foreign language courses. The correlation of success on the MFLAT with good performance in high school foreign language courses was proven over time, and the MFLAT was accepted into academic circles. Though language teachers and a great number of parents had guessed this to be the case for years, the MFLAT showed that having an aptitude for languages existed in a measurable sense. In 1983, Howard Gardner of Harvard University published *Frames of Mind* on his Multiple Intelligence Theory, further strengthening aptitude's acceptance into scholarly circles. Summarized in *Multiple Intelligence, the Theory in Practice* (1993, 8–9), Gardner actually labeled proficiency in languages as being one of seven intelligences which are composed of the following: 1) linguistic intelligence; 2) logical-mathematical intelligence; 3) spatial intelligence; 4) musical intelligence; 5) bodily-kinesthetic intelligence; 6) interpersonal intelligence; and 7) intrapersonal intelligence. He based this categorization on the fact that each of these seven intelligences can be physically located in the brain and can also be developed through experience.

Returning to the MFLAT, what do Carroll's foreign language learners in an English-speaking high school setting have in common with multilingual children all over the world in terms of defining aptitude?

The answer is in the definition of language aptitude itself. This definition serves both the English high school student in a foreign language class and the multilingual child living abroad. Skehan (1998) and Carroll and Sapon (1958) write that language aptitude consists of four points which can be summarized as:

1) The talent for finding the "code" or pattern of languages ("Phonetic coding ability which is the capacity to distinguish sounds and to code them for future use");

2) A good mind for relating like-concepts and rules ("Associative memory which is the ability to rapidly learn the meaning of target language words");

3) An understanding of grammar ("Grammatical sensitivity which is the ability to recognize the grammatical function of words in sentences");

4) And good guessing ability ("Inductive language learning which is the ability to infer or induce the rules governing a set of language material").

Foreign language aptitude is easily recognized. Rhama is a former student of mine who is a half-Indian, half-Japanese and speaks Hindi, Japanese, and English with no accent. She said that "it just comes naturally" when I queried her on her abilities. I have stood in awe of those who seem to effortlessly acquire languages. Numerous examples come to mind of acquaintances who have aptitude for foreign languages. Some examples follow to reinforce the role aptitude can play in new language learning.

High Aptitude Learners

During my university years I made a number of good friends who are polyglots. One such friend was born to Lebanese parents but lived in Ecuador. She had attended part of high school in the United States and during her university years studied and later spoke quite fluently in French and Italian. She spoke Arabic and Spanish with no accent and English, French, and Italian with a "purposeful" one (Harding and Riley, 1996, note that some adult multilinguals actually emphasize their accents in foreign languages in order to draw attention to the fact that they are speaking a language which is not native to them). Another example is of a good friend from college who was Italian but had grown up in Paris and attended the American School there. He subsequently fell in love with an Ecuadorian, and by the time I met him he spoke Italian, French, English, and Spanish with a subtle (but also emphasized on his part) accent. Another friend from college was from Haiti and spoke both Creole and French at home. He went to school in the United States and subsequently learned some Spanish, Portuguese, and Italian simply because of his interest and travel. My husband is another case in point. He grew up in Ecuador and attended the German School where he learned English as a third language. He studied French at the Sorbonne in Paris at the university level and then went on scholarship to Japan to learn Japanese as a young diplomat. He speaks these five languages (Spanish, German, English, French, and Japanese) with extremely good grammar but with an accent (that I dare say he is proud of).

While these cases may be enviable, they are not presented here to raise the ire of the reader but rather to illustrate how aptitude functions in language learning. Just like the musician who needs to practice his instrument or the gymnast who has always been great at balance and kinesthetic abilities, the polyglot is born with a talent, or in Gardner's terms, "intelligence." But just as the musician and the gymnast need the chance to practice and have the opportunity to use their skills, the person high in language aptitude needs to use his gift or it could go unnoticed and his potential in language unfulfilled. In the above-mentioned cases these friends had a good number of opportunities to learn and use their many languages due to their leisure travel and education. Someone may be born with great potential to learn languages, but if underused or not used at all, this potential will not flourish. This brings us to the role and importance of a supportive home environment, school setting, and firm community base for the fostering of second language acquisition. But first, a few stories.

SOME SNAPSHOTS OF SUCCESS BASED ON APTITUDE

Rebecca: The New York Jew Who Knew Spanish and German

Rebecca (case TT) was born in Israel and lived in Germany until she was nine years old. She then returned to Israel with her mother, father, and two brothers until she was thirteen. At thirteen the family moved to New York until she was eighteen years old. She speaks Hebrew with no accent as the family spoke it at home when she was little, but due to her high aptitude and auditory inclination, she also speaks with no accent in English, even though she learned it in the Third Window. She says that she was quite fluent in German as a child, but after so many years without use, she says she would have to "start from scratch" in order to feel comfortable speaking it again. She can read in German, English, and Hebrew fluently, though she says she has to work at writing in German. She studied Spanish for a time during her high school years in New York and says she feels she has a talent for languages. Interestingly enough, her three children have not followed her linguistic footsteps and speak primarily in Hebrew. The family did spend a year in Boston when the children were three, seven, and nine years old. She says that her oldest son benefited the most from his English exposure in the public school system. He had no trouble speaking when they left a year later, though he struggled with the written aspect of the language. The middle child was seven at the time and shy by nature. Rebecca says that he did not use much English, but is better at writing it than his older brother. Rebecca's rather shy three-year-old daughter would sing in English, but did not speak it very much, but then again, she "doesn't say very much in Hebrew" either. Rebecca feels that it is very important for the children to know English, as it will serve them later in life in their university studies or in looking for a job. She also feels very close to the United States as her adolescence was spent there. Her husband is bilingual in English and speaks to the children in Hebrew. Rebecca admits that there was a lack of strategy in getting her children to use English, mainly because she felt it was not as "natural" as speaking to them in Hebrew, as they were born in Israel and were surrounded by Hebrew speakers. She feels strongly, however, that their one-year experience in Boston, and the fact that the children now receive English at school, will lead to their fluency in English in a few years' time.

Rebecca learned German and Hebrew in her First Window and she learned English and Spanish in the Third Window. Her children are monolingual in Hebrew with a passive understanding of English. Hebrew differs greatly from English, making it understandable that the children did not find English easy to learn at first. While Rebecca feels strongly about her ties to English, it is not clear if the children share such a motivation to learn the language. Rebecca's high aptitude for languages and the fact that she is auditorily inclined were the key ingredients in her language success.

Eileen: A Multilingual Irish Mother Passes on Her Gift

Eileen grew up speaking English at home, but attended a bilingual school in Gaelic in Ireland. She learned to read and write in English at home, and then in Gaelic at school. In her early primary years she had German as a "second" language at school. She attended university in Freiburg, Germany, and then moved with her German husband to Bahrain in the Middle East due to his job posting. Eileen has been very careful to speak to her children only in English, and her husband only speaks to them in German, though the couple mixes when they speak to one another. Eileen is a polyglot (English, Gaelic, German, French, and some Arabic) as is her husband (German, English, Arabic, and some French). Their three children are "perfectly bilingual" and attend the German School. Eileen doesn't feel she is particularly talented in languages, but does acknowledge that it is a "gift" to be able to speak more than one language. She and her husband feel strongly that knowing many languages will be of benefit to their children later in life when it comes to searching for a job, but more importantly, being able to communicate with their relatives and knowing and appreciating people from other backgrounds.

Eileen learned Gaelic in the Second Window, German in the Second and Third Windows, and French in the Third Window. Gaelic, interestingly enough, has a geographical relationship to both English and French but not a linguistic one. Gaelic is actually a Celtic language, meaning it is neither of the same families as English and German (Germanic), nor French (Romance). This means that there was no positive linguistic relationship between her languages to account for learning ease.

As in her own experiences, she has been careful to delineate the use of each language with her own children (case WWWW). Such consistency and conscious strategy has been a key factor in her children's successful multilingualism. The children all learned English and German in their First Windows and French in the Second Windows. In her own case, her high aptitude and keen interest in the languages that surrounded her have been pivotal to her language success.

Karen: The "Natural" Swedish-French-English Polyglot

Another example includes a Swedish-Swiss couple (case TTTT) who speak Swedish and French at home and whose three children speak English at school. The parents are both polyglots (father: French and English; mother: Swedish, English, and French). The mother feels that the children have a certain talent for languages as they speak all three with "good" accents. The children read and write in English, which they were taught at school. While the mother says that her children have not been taught reading skills in their other languages at home, they can read in French and Swedish "due to all the books" they have "around the house." The mother feels that her children must learn English as well as Swedish "to have a good life" but she is not concerned about how proficient they become in French.

Karen's children learned their languages in both the First (Swedish and French) and Second (English) Windows. The parents have used the one-parent, one-language strategy consciously and left the third language to the school. Their talent for languages has been very important, but other ingredients, such as opportunity, have also played their role. The family clearly took advantage of the two languages at home, complimenting them with the community's dominant language, which is also one of the parents' languages (French). Additionally, they were able to enroll the children in the international school in English, adding the third language formally. Linguistically, all three are Indo-European languages, and both Swedish and English are part of the Germanic sub-family and share some similarities. There are two girls and one boy in the family and all speak equally well, though Karen's son was slower to start speaking, she says. All the children are right-handed.

While their high aptitude has been perhaps the pivotal factor in their language learning, they have taken full advantage of the opportunities of the language of the environment (French) and school (English) to grow from being merely proficient bilinguals to proficient multiliterates.

The Vásquez Family: Brothers Born in Korea, Speaking Spanish, and Who Went to School in English and French

Another family is made up of an Ecuadorian couple (case CC) whose sons were born in Korea. Upon returning to Ecuador the elder attended the American School briefly before the family was sent to Belgium and then Switzerland, where both children began schooling in French. The parents are polyglots (father: Spanish, some English, some French, and some Italian; mother: Spanish, English, and French). The mother speaks to the children in a mixture of Spanish (mostly), English ("so they won't forget what they learned in grade school"), and French (depending on the company present). If an English-speaker is present, the mother often addresses the children in English. The father speaks to the children in Spanish. The mother feels that the older son has a high aptitude for language, but that her younger son does not. The older son can read proficiently in Spanish, French, and some English. The younger son, who is five, is learning to recognize letters and letter sounds in French in school. The family goal is for the children to maintain their English as it is "the most useful language in the world," and that they are functional and successful in their French schooling. The mother thinks that it is important for them to learn to read and write in Spanish, and that her older son can do so with some amount of concentration, but she has not formally taught them to do so at home.

The two right-handed boys learned Spanish and had exposure to Korean in the First Window. The older boy learned English in the Second Window and French in the Second and Third Windows. The younger boy learned French in the Second Window. The family speaks Spanish amongst themselves. Both children have a rather high level of English, though this is mainly due to exposure through the media (television, videos, and movies). French and Spanish being similar (both Romance languages) has been helpful. The older child's confident personality has aided with the way he aggressively pursues language. The younger child realizes the importance of doing his best and wishes to please his parents, so he tries hard, being motivated by those two factors. As a reflection of their mother mixing languages, the children do the same, but only in her presence. Their languages have been a direct result of their family moves from Korea to Ecuador to Belgium to Switzerland, and the Opportunity such a lifestyle has presented.

The mother's mixing of languages has been overshadowed by her older son's aptitude and the great many opportunities he has to use his languages. His high motivation is due to a desire to "fit in" with the local children and to be able to succeed in school.

All of these stories in some way illustrate the importance of aptitude in language learning, but also highlight other factors in our recipe. This leads us to the next important element we can cultivate, Motivation, which follows in chapter 4, *Baking Instructions*.

_____ *Chapter 4* _____

Baking Instructions

"READ DIRECTIONS CAREFULLY BEFORE YOU BEGIN"

I think just about every recipe I've ever read, from box-cake mixes to fancy French pastries, all forewarn the cook that they must "read the directions carefully before they begin." As a child I wondered if this was in contrast with reading it *after* I had begun, or was it opposed to skimming and not really "reading," or perhaps reading very quickly as opposed to "carefully." In any case, such directions are vital to a successful recipe. If I only tell you that the ingredients include flour, sugar, milk, and eggs, but do not explain when and how to mix them, you would not be sure if you were baking a pancake, a cookie, or a crêpe. When you read the directions, you know how the ingredients are mixed, and can be assured of a delicious outcome.

When raising multilingual children, our *Baking Instructions* include the definitions and uses of Motivation, Strategy, and Consistency. These three factors take the "what" of ingredients (the Windows and Aptitude), and tell us "how" they need to be used. Read on, *carefully*.

THE ROLE OF MOTIVATION IN LANGUAGE ACQUISITION

Many studies and whole theories of language learning revolve around the concept of motivation. One's personal desire to learn a language can be a most powerful factor, and one that you, the parent, have partial control over when helping your child. Motivation can come in positive forms and in negative forms and can come from internal and external sources. The place of motivation in the family (from the child and from parents) is discussed here, and the role of the school and community motivation is shown in more detail in the ingredient of "Opportunity" (chapter 5).

Self-motivation can come about when someone wants to learn because of personal goals. This can occur when someone falls in love with a speaker of another language, for example. This also takes place with children when they want to be able to play with the foreign-language-speaking neighbors, or when television cartoons can only be received in the second language.

Parents can help motivate their children through encouragement and by setting an example. Examples can take many forms ranging from attempting to learn the language yourself, to reading in the foreign language in front of the child, to showing respect for the foreign language via the culture. Parents can be supportive of their child's attempts to learn the foreign language, offering praise when new words are learned and vocalizing awe at the child's learning speed. Parents do not have to be linguists to aid their children in language development. By offering a caring environment, a good book to snuggle up with, and enthusiasm for their own language, they are already helping a great deal.

I know many mothers and fathers who chalk up success or failure in learning a language to a child's motivation to do so. "He's good because he wants to be good; he's bad because he wants to be bad." In most cases, parents have good reason to feel the way they do. Motivation—both internal and external—is a key variable, though in isolation it serves little. A child who is highly motivated but who has no opportunity to learn will get nowhere. Similarly, a child who has no motivation and is force-fed a language will probably also have little success. *Wanting* to learn is a key part of the process and a good reflection of the product. *Liking* the language, the language teacher, or the things the language brings the child are also important.

John Schumann (1997) writes in *The Neurobiology of Affect in Language* that people learn differently and have different levels of success depending on what value the language has for them, and depending on their relationship to the speakers of that language. A young child who desperately wants to play with the neighborhood kids who speak in Italian is much more likely to pick up the language than the university student who has been told he must take four units of a foreign language to graduate. Similarly, falling in love with someone who speaks another language can create a strong motivation for learning, as would the opposite effect if you hated your language teacher. This also gives rise to the "logic" behind certain language teaching schemes. The "sink-or-swim" method or "total immersion," where you are tossed into the sea of another tongue and either use it or drown, has a strong motivational foundation. The question of whether negative motivation has the same results as positive motivation (falling in love) can probably be answered by any of us who can recall having learned something by force. Continuing our water metaphor, if you were made to learn to swim by being thrown into the water (and you survived to tell), you probably did learn to swim, but hated the process and possibly swimming itself. Equally true, children berated into doing something (*i.e.*, clearing the table after a meal) instead of having a love of the process instilled in them (by turning it into a game, rewarding them with praise, etc.) may have similar end results, but the difference in stress levels for both the children and adults involved is great.

Another perspective revolves around the issue of personality types as well as motivation. While some feel greatly compelled to learn and use whatever words, phrases, and gestures possible to "survive," others avoid "performing" in another language. Some first-time travelers feel compelled to learn every morsel of language in the country where they are traveling because it means finding a place to sleep or a meal to eat. When I was seventeen years old I did some biking over the summer vacation in England and France. Now, in the far north of France, in Brittany, there were very few souls who conversed in English and, that aside, I *wanted* to speak my guidebook French, to be part of the scene, not just the curious tourist. I remember a great flush of pride when I used a simple but polite phrase to request lodging for the night. A companion who had beat me to the owner had been shouting for ten minutes in loud English. Once I spoke in (halting, guidebook) French, the manager's attitude changed completely and he let us stay. I felt deeply proud and was encouraged to try even more phrases. Each time I had a success (was understood), I wanted to do more, and so goes the spiraling effect of affect.

Different people have diverse motivations for wanting to learn a foreign language, but in all cases it is an important factor. In the cases of our multilingual children, feeling good about the new language and relating positive experiences to the language are key to the process. Positive motivation must be cultivated in order for our kids to nurture a good relationship with their learning experiences in the new language.

Many studies on the effectiveness of bilingual education return to the fundamental role of motivation. Language must be functional for the learner and such a function must be obvious to the learner. If the child feels impelled to comprehend, if he desires to speak, if there is some motivation to write, then he will do so. If reading and writing are recognized as useful tools, then the child will work hard to reach those goals. If the second language has a function in the child's life, if it helps him reach the objective of being accepted at school or having someone to play with in the afternoons, he will feel moved to pursue the language.

However, the opposite can occur as well. When my three-year-old son realized that his first teacher in the German School could speak English (he saw her speaking to me), he figured there was no point in pushing himself too hard, because she would understand his English. And sure enough, in those first weeks of school she would break down and speak in English because she thought she was helping. It wasn't until I began using my elementary German on his second teacher that he began to make more effort (we kept the fact that she spoke some English a secret). Had his first teacher spoken solely in German I think Gabriel would have made speedier progress to the speaking stage, being motivated by the fact that he had no English to fall back on. Motivation can work in several ways, and have both positive and negative effects on language.

This leads us to the psychological question: How can one influence motivation?

Positive Motivation

The home environment plays an important role in building up encouragement, respect, and interest in a second language. If the parents care little about learning the local customs and language of a new country, the child will be hard-pressed to cultivate such respect on her own. This extends from attitude to action. Showing parental interest in the language by setting an example also helps, often more than parents want to admit, as it demands effort on their part to learn the new language as well. If able to, parents can read in the new language in front of their children to show their interest in it. If unable to read, taking classes in the new language shows parental interest in the culture and surroundings to their child. Attempting to listen to the news in the new language (not isolating yourself to what you can find in your own tongue), and speaking whatever limited version of the language you can produce in front of your child (while at the supermarket or gas station, for example), encourages her own use of the language. All this can work towards forming a healthy respect for the new language in your child's mind and fosters her own motivation to learn it. While this puts some burden of the child's success at acquiring a foreign language on the parents' shoulders, it is a realistic expectation. If we want our children to be multilingual and to go through the sometimes arduous process of learning the language, then we need to be willing to do that as well, at least to a certain extent.

While many parents may not have a strong interest in the language per se, they find it necessary to study it to be able to help their children with subjects in school. I have a Swiss-*Romande* (French-speaking) friend who does not really think she needs to learn German for German's sake, but as her son is entering first grade and starting to learn to read and get homework in German she feels compelled to brush up on her school-book skills as well. Similarly, a Nicaraguan mother joined my German class recently, stating that her sixth-grade daughter will now be getting German in school as well as French. She feels compelled to learn the language to help with her daughter's homework. All of these types of motivation serve as a catalyst towards new learning.

The Role of Affect

Children can be influenced emotionally by experiences early in life which can impact their future language learning abilities. In other words, if one has positive contact with a parent or caregiver in a second language when small, this can create an emotional memory which can help them learn the language in later childhood or adulthood. Even if the child is not brought up as a bilingual, he can be receptive to the emotionally positive motivation of experiences in a second language. A friend of mine once brought up the question as to whether her two-year-old son was getting anything out of being in a French-speaking crèche as both she and her husband spoke Spanish at home and the boy did not show any signs of speaking in French. When probed further she said that he was very happy there, adored the teacher with whom he felt very secure, and that he played contentedly for the two hours a day he was left there. In all likelihood this boy is building up fond emotional memories related to his experience in a French-speaking environment and if it remains a positive exchange for him, he will undoubtedly benefit in his later years when he tries to learn French more formally at school.

Tremblay and Garner (1995) have stated the simple idea that the motivation to learn and to achieve knowledge are interdependent. Desiring to learn helps you learn; in turn, once you've learned something new you are rewarded by having "achieved," giving you even more motivation for further learning, and so on. Again, the effect of affect.

Negative Motivation

Unfortunately, just as one can cultivate language acquisition by positive surroundings, one can damage a child's chances for language acquisition (or any other type of learning for that matter) if he is subjected to trauma or stress. Stress hormones such as cortisol, released to the brain when a child is abused or traumatized, can damage it in such a way that fewer synapses are formed, and it is physically smaller in certain regions (Begley 1997). While this research is based on physical trauma and abuse, many a psychologist can testify to the damage that verbal abuse can have on children as well. Such findings caution us about reprimanding a child for his poor results when he actually may be struggling to learn a second language. I know of a sad case where a mother was so desperate for her child to speak clearly and correctly in Spanish that she told him, "You've got to be stupid not to be able to say that right. If you can't do it in Spanish just say it in French." Needless to say, the boy was probably not inspired to attempt speaking Spanish again for quite awhile, and these studies make you wonder if he could, over a long period of such verbal abuse, suffer irreversible damage, if not physically, then certainly psychologically.

Other comments that can negatively influence children have to do with comparing the performance of siblings. Edith Harding and Philip Riley (1996) and Judith Rich Harris (1998) note that even though children can have the same parents and grow up in similar environments, their experiences are not the same because they are different people receiving different information on different levels (due to age differences), and that comparing abilities is never helpful, especially in front of the children involved. Hearing your mother repeatedly comment to her friends that you are not as talented as your brother at languages will certainly take its toll on your motivation level and should be avoided at all costs. And now, some stories illustrating the role of motivation in foreign language learning.

SNAPSHOTS OF HIGH AND LOW MOTIVATION

Marie: The Unwilling French-English Bilingual

Near us live a Swiss-French couple (case S) with a bilingual daughter in French and English (attributed to her paternal grandmother, who is British). The parents are both polyglots (father: French and English; mother: French, English, Spanish, and Italian). The seven-year-old girl attends the local Swiss French-speaking school and is very proficient in oral French and English but says she "hates" school. Her father does not think she is particularly talented in languages. She reads in both French (school) and English (thanks to the grandmother) but is better in English. This could be because her grandmother began teaching her reading skills in English before French was introduced, or equally possible is the child's dislike of the French-speaking school. The girl watches a lot of television and movies in English. The parents did not consciously decide to raise their daughter bilingually. The school and home environment are French. The strength of her English is due almost entirely to the work of her grandmother and the fact that she spends such a great amount of time in her care. This positive attachment to English through her grandmother is in stark contrast to her dislike of her French-speaking school.

In Marie's case, she learned both French and English in the First

Window, and her grandmother was one of her primary caregivers as both parents worked. The family did not consciously decide on a strategy, though the grandmother only speaks in English, the mother in French, and the father uses a mixture of the two with his daughter. Marie is a right-handed female with no siblings. Her unfortunate relationship with school has probably kept her from excelling in French in the same way as she has mastered English literacy skills.

Marie's low level of motivation and her parents' lack of strategy have had a profound, negative impact on the way she views her bilingualism. With any luck her school situation will improve, and with a more consistent dose of French in a more positive environment she will grow to appreciate the benefits of that language as well.

Lila: Leaving All of China Behind, but Learning American Sign

When Lila's parents left China for California they had no intention of ever going back. They told their children they wanted them to "be Americans" and to speak in English (even if they themselves could not at the time). Lila is the fourth of five children, and only the eldest learned Cantonese properly. All of the other children were passive learners in the sense that they heard their parents speaking to each other all the time, and understood when they were spoken to in Cantonese, even though their parents wanted them to respond in English. Lila (case FFFF) was good at languages, however, and learned Cantonese despite being discouraged to do so. In high school she also took Spanish, and was "very good" at it at the time, though she does not feel she speaks it well now due to the lack of practice. In her university studies she took up American Sign Language and became very proficient. This is an unusual case where the parents did not want their child to become bilingual. Perhaps due to her general talent for languages, Lila succeeded despite their discouragement. Her own explanation is that since Cantonese was "all around her" and she heard her parents speaking daily, she was able to passively learn the language and actively use it later in life.

Lila was exposed to Cantonese and learned English in the First Window. She studied Spanish and American Sign Language in the Third Window. Since she had a regular, steady diet of Cantonese, despite being discouraged to learn it, and because she had a good ear, she is still able to use it today. Cantonese, English, and American

Sign are distinct languages (though they do share word order). Lila is a right-handed female who speaks in English with her four siblings. This is one case where low motivation was balanced by a high level of aptitude. Though discouraged from languages initially, Lila's internal motivation gave way to her high aptitude for languages to help her learn Spanish and American Sign, and the opportunity of having a daily diet of Cantonese aided in her ability to maintain that language as well.

Oh Canada! The Strong English, Weak French Bilingual Family

Across the street is a Canadian couple (case N). The parents are both English-French bilingual. The children will get both English and French at school. Having just come from Canada, the children's letter recognition skills in English seem phenomenal when compared with the local children who learn these skills later in school. At four years old the middle child knew all her letters and sounded out many words. The nine-year-old reads quickly and effortlessly in English, but has yet to learn French, which will come later in the international school she attends. The mother feels it is extremely important for children to be able to "think well" in their native tongue before venturing into other languages, but feels that her older daughter has reached a sufficient level of understanding to be able to do just that, and so she will begin French this year in the Third Window. In fact, she entered the French section of the international school in order to expedite her learning and satisfy her curiosity of the language. The parents were happily surprised that she "fit right in" and has not had any complaints about being in an all-French environment. The middle child will learn French in the Second Window and the youngest— who will presumably have exposure if not learn the language outright—will have French once she begins attending a crèche at two-and-a-half. From the parents' perspective, as English now serves as the dominant language in commerce and diplomacy and the children have a firm grounding in it, "it can't hurt" to learn another language (French).

The children seem keen on learning French, though it's difficult to say whether or not they have aptitude for foreign languages as they've never undertaken one before. They are, however, extremely literate in their native English and they appear motivated to learn now that the opportunity has presented itself with their parents' posting to Geneva. The two older girls are right-handed, while the youngest favors her left hand.

The older daughter's internal motivation and her probable aptitude for languages, coupled with the family's opportunity of being overseas in a French-speaking environment, will probably lead to successful bilingualism and multiliteracy skills in this case.

We now turn to the key factor of Strategy which can either enhance or hamper a family's progress towards a multilingual household.

SECOND LANGUAGE LEARNING STRATEGIES

Fondue is a Swiss dish in which three kinds of cheese are melted together in a special ceramic pot and eaten by dipping small pieces of bread into the hot liquid. I laughed out loud when I read the recipe instructions for the first time. It insisted that the cheese be mixed by "moving a wooden spoon in a figure-eight." What would happen if I used a plastic spoon in a circle instead? I did. The fondue just did not taste the same. Something similar happens when deciding just what language strategy to use in our families. No strategy is like not stirring the cheese at all. Using a plastic spoon is like using less than a perfect strategy; it may work, but the end result will not turn out as well as "a wooden spoon in a figure-eight." This is the importance of strategy. Back to the recipe.

Now what about the group of people who introduced language at the right time, had reasonable aptitude, and were motivated, but did not have successful results? I challenge parents in this case to honestly reflect on their children's lives and determine whether or not they introduced the languages with a consistent strategy. For example, parents who switch languages themselves (due to a change of country, for example) can confuse children. Parents, caregivers, or even teachers who are not competent in a certain language and who expose children to grammatical and syntax errors will pass along this lack of language understanding to the children around them. It is as simple as that. Not only is timing crucial, as in using the Windows of Opportunity to your advantage, but being consistent in the way children are taught a second language is vital. This leads us to what strategies are available for parents wanting to help foster the growth and mainte-nance of a second language.

The Method Behind the Madness: Choosing a Language Strategy

Many years ago, I found a very useful book on the subject of bilin-gual family strategies: *The Bilingual Family, A Handbook for Parents* by Edith Harding and Philip Riley (1996). In straightforward terms they begin by looking at what children use language for (building up rela-tionships, exchanging information, thinking, playing with words, etc.) to set the stage for how bilingualism can best be cultivated. The sec-ond part of their book offers sixteen case studies of families who have chosen to raise their children in a bilingual setting, and their varying levels of success with the endeavor. It is from these cases that they developed a typology of bilingual families. My own interpretation amplifies their work to include a total of seven strategies as seen in Figure 4.1.

Looking at the chart, it is painful to admit that as a family we employed not just one, but many of the strategies listed here, as we bumbled our way into being a truly multilingual household. Having very little guidance, it seems that we tried almost all of the popular strategies cited here. We began with the one-parent, one-language strategy when our first child was born (Strategy One): I spoke in English and my husband in Spanish while we lived in Ecuador. Then we switched and both spoke Spanish at home and let the environment take care of the second language, which was English, when we moved from Quito to Boston (Strategy Two). We then tried having the "sec-ond" (really third at the time) language-use being employed in strate-gic situations, as when the children went to a friend's house to play in German, while we lived in an English-speaking environment but spoke Spanish at home (Strategy Seven). Having learned a great deal from these experiments in strategy, we have returned to Strategy One, one-parent, one-language, which has yielded the best results. Since arriving in Geneva, we have added the use of "Place" to define the boundaries of French. My daughter takes ballet and music classes in French after school and she associates those places with that language. One of the great impetuses for this book was that we made our way in a trial-and-error method and suffered some negative consequences in the case of our second child, which I will relate in greater detail

Figure 4.1
Family Language Strategies

	Parent 1	Parent 2	Community	Plan
Strategy 1	Language A (some B)	Language B (some A)	Language A or B	The parents each speak their native language to their child.
Strategy 2	Language A (some B)	Language B (some A)	Language B	Both parents speak Language A to the child who is only fully exposed to Language B when outside the home, and particularly when in school.
Strategy 3	Language A	Language A	Language B	The parents speak their native language to the child and leave the second language to the environment and school.
Strategy 4	Language A	Language B	Language C	The parents each speak their native language to their child who learns a third language from the environment.
Strategy 5	Language A Language B	Language A	Language A	One of the parents always addresses the child in his or her non-native, second language.
Strategy 6	Language A Language B	Language A Language B	Language A	The parents speak their native language to their child except during specific times, such as meals, when they speak the second language.
Strategy 7	Language A	Language A	Language A	Parents speak their native language. The child associates the second language with a certain place, such as special classes or trips to visit relatives.

when discussing the ingredient of "Consistency." If we can spare even one other family from having to experiment with their child's language development, this book will have served its purpose.

SNAPSHOTS OF RECIPES USING OR MISSING A GOOD STRATEGY

The Chaptal Family: A Conscious Separation of Four Languages

Case M is of a family made up of a Spanish mother, a Swiss father, and their two sons. The parents are both bilingual in Spanish and French. The mother speaks to her children in Spanish and her husband speaks to them in French. The children attend a local Swiss French-speaking school and now have German as a "second" language. The children have learned some English from vacations, movies, videos, and television. They speak fluently in French and Spanish and read and write in French and some Spanish. The mother says her children have as much aptitude for languages as "the average Swiss" who has to learn a second or third language in school. She always "assumed" that her children would become bilingual and they chose the one-person, one-language strategy because it was "logical." So far they have had the excellent results they expected.

The two right-handed boys learned French and Spanish in the First Window and German in the Third Window. While they do not speak much English, their comprehension is exceptional, especially given that their exposure to it has been primarily through the media which they gained in both the Second and Third Windows. French and Spanish are both Romance languages with Latin roots and are very similar. German and English share roots as well, perhaps explaining some of the ease that the children have had with their languages.

The parents' careful separation of Spanish and French as a strategy and the children's high aptitude have been the key factors in their success. Opportunity plays a smaller role in this family's case since they have lived in French-speaking Switzerland all of their lives.

The Boy Who Was Bilingual for School Only

Case AA is of a Swiss couple who have placed their children in the German school. The parents are polyglot (father: French, English, and some German; mother: French, English, and some German). The family speaks French at home and the children learn reading and writing skills with the mother at home in French in an organized and methodological way several hours weekly. The elder son is presently learning reading and writing in German at school. The mother does not think her youngest son has much aptitude for languages ("He learned just one word the entire first year of German pre-school!" she claims). Her first son is more outgoing and has better aptitude than his brother, she believes. He speaks fluently in German, having spent the last three years in that school environment. The parents want the boys to learn German in the event they ever have to move to Germany or the German-speaking section of Switzerland because of their job situation. They also chose the German system because they were "not very impressed with the Swiss school system" in their community. For the moment, the only source of German they have is from school, and the mother is beginning to worry if this is sufficient for the younger child.

The French-speaking boys learned their German in the Second Window. The parents have always spoken French exclusively to their children and to each other. Both boys are right-handed. Over the summer they hired a German high school student to play with the boys several hours a day to ensure they would not forget their German over the holidays. The parents are considering increasing their sons' exposure to German by adding extra classes after school.

These boys were monolingual from birth and their environment has remained so. The parents have clearly delineated where French is spoken (home) and where German is spoken (school), and these two do not mix. Since the boys have little opportunity to speak German outside school this language has improved slowly, though improved it has. As the children have no German-speaking relatives to push their learning, and as everything in their world is in French except school, the family has relied on the teachers as a source of inspiration with mixed results. The older boy's present teacher is well-liked by the child and she seems to be getting through to him, impressing upon him and his classmates the need to improve good reading and writing skills in German. With her continued support he should persist in his climb towards successful bilingualism.

The Kurtz Family: Parents Who Mix, Have Children Who Mix

Other friends have cases that are relatively complex to describe. One such situation (case C) is of a family made up of a Colombian-Swiss mother who is part British through her maternal grandmother. Her husband is a Swiss-German. The parents are polyglots (father: German, French, English, some Spanish, and some Japanese; mother: Spanish, French, German, English, and some Japanese). The parents speak German to each other and live in French-speaking Geneva. The mother speaks to her three sons in a mixture of Spanish, French, German, and English. Her sons speak in a mixture of all four languages, though have greater fluency in French (due to school) and, if offered a choice, play with their bilingual (Spanish-French) friends in French. Amongst themselves they mix their languages as well. The eldest, who is seven, has yet to learn to read and recognizes just a handful of letters and their sounds. The mother does not feel that her children are particularly gifted with languages. Both she and her husband found learning languages relatively easy, and assumed that it would come "naturally" to their children, though this has not been the case.

The three boys are all right-handed. While the three children have been exposed to all four languages (French, German, Spanish, and English) in the First Window, they received such exposure in a inconsistent mix, without a conscious strategy. School has offered one form of language consistency (French) as has their caregiver (Spanish). Over the past year the parents have tried to incorporate the one-person, one-language strategy as they now realize their mixing has been passed on to their children.

The boys' mixed results with their languages is due in great part to the parents' lack of strategy and consistency. School will probably contribute to alleviating some of the inconsistencies in their language life and, as mentioned earlier, the parents are now trying to revert to a one-parent, one-language strategy. Both of these things will aid the boys in "untangling" their tongues, hopefully escaping the bane of "semilingualism," and becoming more fluent in the future.

We now turn to Strategy's bedfellow: Consistency.

BEING CONSISTENT WITH THE CHOSEN STRATEGY

In opening the doors (or windows) to a second language for your child you are engaging in the development of a skill that will serve him for a lifetime. As in all new learning, children need to know that their parents approve, support, and will encourage them. However, a word of caution here for the zealous, try-anything-once parent. Part of being a supportive parent is to know your own limits.

It is not recommended to try and help your child with a language you are unfamiliar with. Instead, take the time to go out and take a class yourself, encourage friendships with speakers of language X, or if resources permit, find a tutor who can speak to your child with a native understanding of the language. Cassettes and videos also help, though they could never impart the human closeness of a real native speaker. Why is this so important? If parents are not consistent in the method they use to teach a child a second language, the child will become confused. If the parents, caregivers, or teachers mix languages, they will have children who mix. If you have parents with grammatical fallacies in their spoken language, their children will suffer the same. I learned this crucial point the hard way with my second child.

Had I known then what I know now! While we had been religiously consistent with my daughter and her language development from infancy, we purposely, but inconsistently, switched language strategies when we moved to Boston from Ecuador. Not knowing then what I know now about the Windows of Opportunity for language development and the great importance of consistency by the child's caregivers, I thought we were doing the children a favor by giving sanctuary to Spanish in the home. We believed that since the environment was going to be English, and as Spanish would have only come from a single source, my husband, if we had continued our first strategy of one-person, one-language, then Spanish would not be heard enough by our small children (three-and-a-half and thirteen months) to be maintained. I did not realize the gravity of that decision on the children's language development at the time.

A Case of Inconsistency and the Unfortunate Outcomes

My son, Gabriel, was just over a year old when we decided to all speak in Spanish at home while in Boston, instead of the one-person, one-language strategy we had used in Ecuador. Switching strategies on my son at this crucial developmental stage really sent his mental facilities for a loop. Whereas mommy had always spoken in English and *papi* in Spanish, mommy was now speaking in Spanish and *papi* would often stop on a street corner to chat with classmates in English! I have videos of him when we first arrived in Boston from Quito. At that time he was speaking at age level. Four months later I have a video in which he speaks *less* than he had upon first arriving, and *even less* six months post-arrival. Basically, his second year of life evolved around animal noises and sounds, rather than words, and a lot of physical movement. When we returned to Ecuador a year after our ill-fated decision to switch strategies, and then moved to Switzerland two months later, we returned to our tried and true method of one-person, one-language. Two years after the country, language, and strategy change, at age three, Gabriel started to come into his own. It became clear that he understood nearly everything in Spanish and English with equal comprehension, and most of the things said in German, which is the school language. He slowly emerged from his English-only state and began to speak to his father in Spanish, something he had started to do at thirteen months of age but which had been put on hold for two years while he sorted us all out, especially this crazy mother of his who began his life speaking in one language, then switched on him just as he was understanding the pattern. I have recorded several other cases in which parents admitted mixing languages in the home (and even within the sentences they spoke to their children), and where the language development of the child was delayed. In some rare cases the children "never recovered" and remained "mixers" themselves into late adolescence, at which point they were "straightened out" either due to a rigorous school structure or due to a parent's initiative. But in most cases, once children are offered more consistency in their language intake (either through a return to a single, conscious language strategy, or through the consistency offered from formal schooling), they are able to sort it out and separate the languages. Gabriel's improvement has been rapid and he has shown a Copernican change in his language skills once we began being more consistent. He went from English-only animal noises, to a kind of non-stop chatterbox in four languages. (I recorded notes to myself on a recent car trip that he spoke three-hours-ten-minutes straight in a single, personal narrative!) I expect he will have equally proficient language skills as my other two children, so long as we remain faithful to a single strategy of fomenting multilingualism in our house from now on.

An interesting question is why my oldest child, the three-and-a-half-year-old girl, was not affected adversely though she lived through the same process of strategy change in Boston. I believe it was due to her age. For three-and-a-half years she had lived in a consistent, one-person, one-language situation. She was completely sure of her Spanish and her English before this move and had a good vocabulary in each. She suffered a relapse of mixing languages because she watched me do it all the time and because she was missing some words. It took her about a month upon arrival in Boston to unravel her sentences, and when we returned to Quito at age four-and-a-half it took her a few weeks to settle back into age-level Spanish, but she did so in both cases with little suffering. Her example, and especially that of Gabriel's, is why I feel so strongly about the influence of the Windows of Opportunity and about the issue of consistency.

To complete our story: Our family is presently living in Switzerland, but my husband still speaks to the children in Spanish and I speak to them in English. During story time at night my husband will read in German, if that's the children's choice (as they are in the German School), or I in French if they request a book in that language (as the environment is French). In this way we show our support and respect for the other languages surrounding us, but do not let Spanish or English suffer from neglect.

Practically speaking, I would suggest that if the family has just moved and if the child is already multilingual, the parents should maintain the strategy used before the move (change of countries and languages). Switching languages on a small child, especially with everything else being changed at the same time (house, school, friends, food) can create great confusion and cause extreme stress and even rejection of the language, the country, and the parent, though such rejection is usually temporary. This is a very important point we will see illustrated by the stories which follow.

SNAPSHOTS OF VARYING DEGREES OF CONSISTENCY

The Brazilian-Swiss Neighbors Who Speak German, French, English, and Portuguese at Dinner

There is a family formed by a Brazilian-Swiss couple (case SSSS) who have two teenage boys who grew up hearing Portuguese, French, and Swiss German at home and who received English and French at school. The parents are polyglots (father: German, French, Italian, English, and Portuguese; mother: Portuguese English, French, and some German). The boys have learned to read in French and have been taught some English reading skills in school, but with less success. The boys speak in French and Portuguese without an accent, but they speak German and English haltingly. Their parents say that the second son has more aptitude for foreign languages than the first, who is also extremely shy, but they acknowledge that they have an exceptional "load" with four languages and a lot of mixture at home. The parents both stress the need to be multilingual "in today's world." The father's gift for languages has served him greatly in his job career, he feels.

The boys learned Portuguese and French, two very similar languages, in the First Window, and had exposure to German at that time as well, though less consistently. English was introduced in the Second Window when they began school. The parents find that certain languages express certain sentiments better, so they find they mix their languages with frequency. English is a Germanic language, but has been enriched by a lot of Latin words which are also found in French, making the three languages complementary in their family situation. The two boys are right-handed.

Though these children have had a great opportunity to learn their languages due to their parents' native tongues, the environment, and their international schooling during crucial moments in their lives, they have not undertaken the challenge of multilingualism in a consistent strategy, which has slowed their progress towards true multiliteracy skills. As their languages are a part of their daily lives, albeit in a mixed fashion, they have the great possibility of becoming fluent polyglots over time, but the process is slower than it needed to be due to the lack of consistency.

The Cárdenas Family: A Monolingual Home with Multilingual Children

The neighbors across the park are Nicaraguan (case UUUU). The mother is a polyglot who speaks Spanish and English, with no strong accent, basic French, and is learning German. The girls' adoptive father speaks Spanish, some English, and a little French. The family speaks Spanish as well as English at home due to the length of time the mother and daughters lived in the United States. In school, the older daughter, now in the sixth grade, is taught French and receives German as a "second" language, but she is struggling. Having just arrived in Switzerland last year she was faced with learning French by immersion. And just one year afterwards, German. As a result of this demanding challenge she will repeat a year in order to improve her language skills. Failing a grade and feeling little or no motivation to learn the languages, as her family's stay in Switzerland is only temporary, has given little encouragement to her efforts. Her mother does not think she has much talent for languages but believes it is more a question of "being lazy" than having or not having aptitude for languages. The girl knew how to read and write in English before coming here, but her mother is very worried that those language skills are "being forgotten" because of the lack of practice. The mother is very concerned that the children maintain their English skills, though they have less exposure to this language now, so she speaks to them in a mixture of English and Spanish. She is not so concerned about perfecting skills in French as "it will not serve them as much as the English" later in life. The mother admits that multilingualism is a necessity in her family's case, given the moves they will likely make throughout her daughters' upbringing.

The two girls learned English and Spanish in the First Window. The younger girl learned French in the Second Window (age seven) and the older daughter is in the process of learning French and German in the Third Window (age eleven). While their natural father always addresses them in English and their adoptive father always addresses them in Spanish, the mother mixes Spanish and English, depending on the situation. The girls have plenty of opportunity and necessity to practice their oral and written French, but they do not have a great deal of motivation for either French or German, however, as they do not see their long-term usefulness. French's similarity to Spanish has been a great asset academically. The girls are both right-handed and speak English to each other.

The older girl's limited success with her third (French) and fourth (German) languages is due entirely to opportunity. She had little motivation to learn (except the threat of failing the year again) and she heard many of her languages in a mixed manner with little strategy or consistency. She was lucky enough to have learned Spanish and English in the First Window, however, giving her something to fall back on when learning the somewhat related languages of French (to Spanish) and German (to English).

The Heinle Family: From Every Corner of the Earth and Every Angle of the Mouth

The Heinle Family (case A) is formed by a Colombian-German couple whose first child was born in Vienna. When she was nine months old the family moved to New York, and her mother believes her daughter's first words were in English, though this is neither of her parents' native languages. The parents are both polyglots (father: German, English, Spanish, and some French; mother: Spanish, English, German, and French). Their son was born in New York a year-and-a-half later. The family then moved to Malaysia when their daughter was three-and-a-half years old and the son was nearly a year-and-a-half old. Two years later they moved to Switzerland where the children began formal schooling in the German School. The children now also receive extra French classes at school. The mother speaks to the children in a mixture of mainly Spanish, some English, and some German. The German father speaks to them in English. The older child is learning to read and write in German at the moment. The son, who is five, is beginning to learn to recognize letters and write in English. The mother feels her daughter has language aptitude and her son has a great passive knowledge of languages, but not for speaking, but she feels strongly that he "is absorbing the languages around him, and when he's older he will be able to speak" well in all of his languages.

The daughter received German and Spanish in the First Window, and English from nine months to three-and-a-half years old. She was exposed to English, Malay, Chinese, and German in the Second Window. The younger son was exposed to English, Spanish, and some

German in the First Window. Between eighteen months and three-and-a-half years old he was surrounded by English, Malay, and Chinese as well. He then learned German in the Second Window when he began attending school. Since the father usually addresses the children in English, school was the boy's first consistent exposure to German. Curiously enough, the children speak to each other primarily in English, though they often invent words which sound English, though are in reality German or Spanish. Given a "pure" language environment, as when they went on holiday to Colombia and where everyone spoke Spanish (including their parents), they too became more consistent in their language usage. The same seems to be occurring in the school environment, which should hopefully aid in their complete separation of languages. Both children are right-handed. The parents admit they never consciously decided upon a language strategy, though they both feel confident that their children will sort it out with time.

The son has been very lucky to have had exposure to a large number of languages at crucial periods in his development. However, due to the generally inconsistent manner with which he received his languages, his learning has been greatly passive up to the present. He does have, however, a deep desire to learn his parents' languages (Spanish and German), to do well at school (German), to communicate with his sister and friends (English), and understand the media that surrounds him (English and French). This high level of motivation, plus the consistency that school is now offering him, should help him eventually reach proficient levels of multilingualism, as his mother has projected.

We now turn to the *Kitchen Design*, that is, within what framework we are doing all this cooking. The next chapter asks each family to think about what Opportunities they have surrounding them, what the Relationship is between the languages that their child is learning, and to look at the impact that Siblings may have on the child language learner.

———————————— *Chapter 5* ————————————

Kitchen Design: The Role of the Language Environment

THE LAY OF THE LAND

Do you have lots of counter space in your kitchen? Too few cupboards to store things, or many? A great variety of pots and pans or just one? The way your kitchen is designed has an influence on the environment in which you create your delicacies. This is not to say that scrumptious marvels cannot be produced out of a hole-in-the-wall kitchen and that Julia Child's kitchen always produces winners (though this is usually the case). However, things can be made easier when baking in a space with good facilities and room to let your inventive spirit run wild.

Everyone's lasagna tastes different. Isn't that funny? How can Aunt Jane, mom, and granny get together, all use the "same" recipe and their lasagnas come out tasting different from each other? Two things contribute to this. As we saw earlier, each family mixes the ingredients in slightly different proportions, which has an effect on the outcome and, secondly, our kitchens are equipped differently. Aunt Jane has an electric oven, mom uses gas, and granny bakes on wood. Aunt Jane has Teflon, mom uses a glass dish, and granny uses metal. Aunt Jane has an electric cheese grater, mom has a manual one, and granny uses a knife. Every little difference alters the final taste just slightly, and that is why there are as many ingredient combinations possible as there are multilingual families.

Such tools play a great role in your child's ability to learn a new language, just as good cooking utensils can facilitate the preparation of a meal. Sure, you can still fire up the chimney and dump everything into an old pan and cross your fingers, hoping that it all turns out edible. But modern facilities like stick-proof pans, blenders, and convection ovens have made things a lot easier for the cooks of today. And so will an understanding of the language learning environment ease your move into the multilingual world. Raising multilingual children is done in a specific language environment. How that environment is defined is what we turn to next.

WHAT IS YOUR FAMILY LANGUAGE ENVIRONMENT?

While every family is unique, families interested in raising multilingual children generally reflect one of the situations below:

- **Monolingual family in a same-language environment** (The Smiths speak English and live in the USA but believe in the importance of more than one language.)
- **Monolingual family in a different-language environment** (The Joneses speak English within their family, but live abroad due to a job posting; the Changs speak Chinese but have emigrated to America.)
- **Bilingual family in a same-language environment** (The Barrellas speak Italian and Spanish at home and live in a Spanish environment.)
- **Bilingual or Multilingual family in a different-language environment** (The Espinosas speak English and Spanish at home but live in a French environment.)

Whether the family situation is one of a diplomat abroad, a new immigrant, expatriate, or that of a highly motivated monolingual family in a same-language environment, it is important to recognize that each family will "mix" their ingredients in different ways given their environment. Each of these environments offers different kinds of opportunities, which we turn to next.

WHAT ARE THE OPPORTUNITIES IN YOUR ENVIRONMENT?

L. S. Vygotsky (1896–1934) was a Soviet thinker and educator who believed that language is the tool through which society transmits its knowledge and its values to the child. In other words, language is how adults socialize children. Thought, he believed, is guided by speech. How one chooses to speak and what language he is able to use are elements resulting in how society is eventually formed (Vygotsky 1985, preface). The bottom line is that the language of a given society reflects the needs of that society; we have all the words we need for the type of society we live in.

This is interesting to reflect on while I sit here in Switzerland writing. What are the needs of this society, for example? Within Switzerland, with its four regions and four official languages, there are a great number of possibilities for linguistic and cultural insights. In addition, geographically speaking, if I drive four minutes west I am in France. If I go north some three hours I am in Germany. If I travel east for four-and-a-half hours I arrive in Italy, and some five hours to the northeast and I am in Austria. England is an hour away by plane and Denmark, Sweden, and Finland just two. Being in Switzerland, in "the heart of Europe," adds to Vygotsky's idea that the words we use meet the needs of our society, but in this case, the words come from several languages.

At a recent ministerial-level conference of the European Community in Brussels the average number of languages spoken by the ministers was four each. Even the current British Prime Minister, Tony Blair, recently addressed French Parliament in French, breaking the long-standing tradition of presentations by anglophones solely in English. These examples serve to show the multilinguistic needs of those residing in Europe at the beginning of the twenty-first century.

Similarly, a country's physical size and linguistic isolation can create the need to learn another language. Some examples include Japan, Thailand, and Korea in which moderate-sized countries are isolated by the languages they speak. Nowhere in the world do they speak Japanese but in Japan, Thai but in Thailand, or Korean but in Korea. If the Japanese, Thais, and Koreans want to be part of the changing "globalization" they either have to inspire others to study their language, or learn a new one themselves. But back to my kitchen in Geneva.

I pull out a carton of juice from the refrigerator. "Orange Juice" is written in French, Dutch, and Portuguese, as are the ingredients. I carry both Swiss and French currency in my wallet and find some German coins from a recent visit over the border there as well. Contact with other languages is a daily occurrence here, and so the needs of this society are very different from those of people in countries such as the United States, for example. In the U.S. it is possible to travel the width and length of the country for hours, days, or even weeks (or an entire life!) and never have to speak anything but English. But for those Americans living in multilingual communities, as in most of the southwest (Texas, Arizona, New Mexico, or California) or eastern cities like New York, or for those who travel abroad, a change in the community also changes language needs.

Philosophically, this leads us to the greater question of the emerging global society formed of families from different countries who find themselves in communities which are not their "own." If one's language responds to the needs of one's society, as Vygotsky says, and the needs are multiple in the "global village," then perhaps the languages needed are multiple as well. But coming back down to earth for a moment (in my kitchen in Geneva), what is the ideal environment we wish for our multilingual children?

If your family lives in a different language environment you should count yourselves lucky. Those diplomats or other expatriate families whose companies have "sent" the family abroad have been given a unique opportunity for language learning. When children rely on their new language to make friends and to succeed in school they tend to learn very quickly. When cartoons on television and chatter in the streets offers them the chance to practice their new skills, they are eased into the language through immersion, like a warm bath on a cold rainy day. Children in this situation can become comfortable with the language faster than if only exposed to it in the classroom. The community language influence in some countries is quite strong as well. In Switzerland, for example, where most official signs, the currency, and food labels are in three or four different languages (French, German, Italian, and Romansh), a respect for other languages and sub-cultures within a country is built, though done subtly. If your community has similar tolerance of other language cultures, take advantage of them and highlight their presence for your children so that they realize "they're not alone" in their endeavors to learn more than one language.

While much of Europe is moving in this direction of linguistic expansion due to closer links within the European Community, the United States is as closed as ever in the wide-spread use of other languages. But whereas the U.S. may not offer many chances to read cereal boxes in other languages, the overall tolerance for other languages (for example, the requirement that people be allowed to vote in their native language in California) provides its own opportunities, as do the many students with various cultural backgrounds who make up your child's classroom. Some schools offer after-school language clubs, some communities have activities in other languages, or you may have a neighbor who speaks the language your child is learning (see Appendix A for other suggestions). Some opportunities are obvious, others need to be sought out, but whatever the degree of community support for your child's language endeavors, make the most of what can be found.

If we are at the other extreme, a monolingual family in a same-language environment, our task has been made more complicated, but not impossibly so. It's like being asked to bake a soufflé in a cake dish, or prepare a four-course meal in a small kitchen. Everything is possible, though perhaps not so easy. Creativity is the key, and money does not hurt either. Children who are given the chance to learn a foreign language in the First or Second Windows can benefit from creative school programs or study abroad opportunities. By teaching French to kindergarten children, schools can offer monolingual families the opportunity to incorporate a foreign language into their lives. As we saw in the *Ingredients* and the Windows of Opportunity, such connections in the brain can be retraced later in life to gain complete fluency with future study. If in the Third Window, families who can offer their child the chance to study abroad for a summer (or to visit relatives in another country) will be giving them the "gift of tongues" which will serve them throughout their lives, not only linguistically, but by opening the doors to cultural understanding as well.

The Family, School, and Community Triad will be discussed in further detail in chapter 7, but for now leave it said that when children learn languages beyond the First Window, they and their families must take full advantage of the opportunities in the environment, and where necessary, create some of their own. Some ideas follow.

SNAPSHOTS WHICH TAKE ADVANTAGE OF THE ENVIRONMENT

From South America to South Geneva: The Brazilian-Ecuadorian Who Studied in English, French, and German

There is a family made up of a Brazilian mother and an Ecuadorian father and their four children (case J). The parents are polyglots (father: Spanish, Portuguese, and English; mother: Portuguese, Spanish, and French). The family speaks both Portuguese and Spanish together at home. The mother speaks to the children only in Portuguese and the father only in Spanish. They never considered doing it any other way because it would be "unnatural" to talk to their children in a language other than their own mother tongue. The mother feels that all the children have a gift for foreign languages and that their success is highly related to this personal aptitude.

The elder daughter finished high school in an international school in Ecuador which taught in Spanish and English. She studied French upon arriving in Geneva, and then took a qualifying entrance exam for university study which she passed, attesting to her high level of language skills as well as her preparation overall. She also speaks, reads, and writes in English, Spanish, and Portuguese. Their elder son finished high school in one of the international schools in Geneva, then went on to university studies in an American university in Geneva. The younger daughter is attending the local Swiss middle-school in French. She has extra classes in English and is learning German as a subject at school. The younger son is in a pre-school program in French and English. The parents feel strongly that the children need Spanish and Portuguese to be able to communicate with their relatives in their respective countries.

The children learned Portuguese and Spanish in the First Window. The two older children learned English in the Second Window and French in the Third Window. The third child learned French in the Second Window and German in the Third Window. The youngest has an exceptionally high aptitude for languages and in the Window-and-a-Half stage learned a great deal of French and English from his crèche. The children primarily speak Spanish to each other. They are all right-handed. The close linguistic relationship among Spanish, Portuguese, and French has contributed to their success, as has their general aptitude for foreign languages. But the factor of Opportunity has given them the chance to actually make the most of their skills, using each of their languages as part of their daily lives.

While the mother believes that her older daughter's success with languages is due to her high aptitude, I believe that the many opportunities she has had in which to use her languages on a daily basis (living and studying in countries and schools which require a firm command of the languages) has contributed greatly to her success as well.

The Howe Family: Monolingual in a Multilingual Environment

The Howes (case N) are American but are living in French-speaking Geneva and travel extensively during the holidays around the rest of Europe. The daughter is in the Window-and-a-Half and the mother feels she has an exceptional capacity for languages. While only two, she "speaks" a lot of French, understands "everything" and mimics other languages when she hears them. The son is in the Second Window at five-and-a-half, and is not necessarily so talented, his mother says. The parents have recently decided to take the son out of the local French-speaking Swiss school and enroll him in a private English-speaking school because they do not want him to "lag behind his peers" in terms of reading and writing when they return to the United States. They have concerns however, as they want the children to retain the French skills they have "picked up" over the past two years of exposure. After long discussion, the parents decided to engage a French-speaking baby-sitter to watch the children two hours a day after school. By maintaining a consistent diet of French for the coming two years, the projected length of the husband's contract, they hope to ensure that the children's French is retained.

This boy's exposure to the language at a crucial period in his life (the Second Window) was important in planting the seeds for language acquisition; however, the chance to use his language with meaningful caregivers is even more important at this point in helping maintain his French skills.

The Sánchez Family: From Manila to Multilingualism in the Czech Republic

Case O is a fascinating one of a Czech mother and a Philippine father who speak English together. The father is bilingual in Tagalog and English and the mother is a polyglot (Czech, German, French, English, and some Spanish). Their three daughters attended the German School as their maternal grandparents were originally from Germany. The mother speaks to the children in Czech, the father in English and Tagalog. The mother believes that foreign language aptitude is indeed a gift and that, while all her daughters have this gift, the youngest has the most talent, and therefore also took French classes at the local Swiss school. The older children were to learn reading and writing in German in first grade but have since moved to Austria. The parents have decided that instead of a German education, the girls will now attend an English international school as "German will come from the environment." The mother feels that it is vital for the children to be able to read and write and speak perfect English. She feels that they will gain some literacy skills in the other languages "naturally" once they have their footing in English.

The children learned Czech, English, and Tagalog in the First Window. They had exposure to German through visits to relatives' homes in the same. They formally learned German in the Second Window, and the youngest child learned French as well. The three right-handed girls usually speak English to each other, unless in the company of German-speakers, in which case they switch. Both parents, though right-handed, are very "right hemisphere oriented" (creative, artistic, spatially oriented, literary). Czech and Tagalog are very dissimilar languages, but as they were learned in the First Window this posed no problems for the girls. Czech is a Slavic language and German and English of Germanic origin, and Tagalog comes from the Austro-Asiatic group of languages and shares no roots with any of the other languages. The success they have had with their languages is probably due to the combination of aptitude and the opportunity they have had to travel and use their languages in meaningful situations. Living and attending school where the youngest daughter "needed" her languages has given this girl the opportunity to capitalize on her aptitude for foreign languages to learn many distinct ones.

Laura: The Hungarian Who Moved to the Center of the World

Laura met her Ecuadorian husband when they were both studying on scholarship in what was then the Soviet Union. The couple moved briefly to her home in Hungary, then settled in Ecuador after a time. Laura learned Spanish without much trouble (as it was "nothing compared to Russian and Hungarian"), albeit with a strong accent. The couple has two daughters, the elder of whom attends a local private school in Spanish. Laura only speaks to her daughters in Hungarian, and addresses her husband in Hungarian as well. Laura has never learned to write in Spanish, though she "gets by as it is such a phonetic language." She can read in Spanish, though does not do so with much frequency, but she is trying to change this in order to help her daughter with her homework. On family vacations back to Hungary, she says her daughter, who is very shy by nature, takes a few weeks to get comfortable, but then has no trouble speaking with her relatives, who know no Spanish. Laura's primary goal for wanting her daughter to be bilingual (Spanish and Hungarian) is to communicate with these relatives. She says she only spoke to her daughter in Hungarian from birth because it was "logical" to do so.

Laura learned her second and third languages as an adult in the Third Window. Her daughter, however, learned Spanish and Hungarian in her First Window. Spanish (a Romance language) and Hungarian (from the Finno-Ugric family) do not share similar linguistic roots. This appears to have posed no problems for Laura's daughter (case KK) and only a problem of accent for Laura herself. The family's motivation for maintaining Hungarian lies in the strong links to family there. Laura's approach to languages was that of a means towards other ends. She learned Russian to go to university and Spanish in order to fit into her husband's society. In this case, her ability to learn other languages was both part and parcel of Opportunity, first in being able to study and second in being able to relocate without much trouble.

The Polyglots Who Came to Dinner

A final case is not really of a single family, but rather of a type of situation I have been in on a number of occasions which merits listing here as it illustrates the need for multilingualism in today's world. Recently, my husband and I attended a dinner with three other couples. The languages spoken by the couples were:

Couple 1: Spanish-English-German-French-Japanese;
Couple 2: German-English-Gaelic-Arabic-French;

Couple 3: German-English-French;

Couple 4: German-English-Spanish-French.

What was a hostess to do? Before being seated at the table, little cliques would form and conversations were conducted in what was presumed to be the stronger language of the pair or threesome. When I spoke with two other women, whose first languages were Spanish and German respectively, we ended up in English as it was our "common ground." My husband (whose first language is Spanish) joined in happily with the other three men who all spoke German as a first language, and spoke primarily in German accordingly. Chatter in the kitchen was conducted in a mixture of French and German because a recipe from Provence was being discussed by a native English speaker and a Spanish speaker. Taking into account everyone's languages there was the following break-down of possible conversation participants:

German (7 fluently, 1 partially),

Spanish (3 fluently, 1 partially),

French (4 fluently, 4 partially), and

English (8 mixed levels).

Japanese wasn't even considered since it was my husband and I who speak the language (partially, not fluently), and who is going to talk to their own spouse at a dinner party anyway? Energetic exchanges filled the air in all of these languages until we sat down at the table and had to share a conversation in the large group. A deathly silence filled the room momentarily. Who was going to speak first, and in what language? And should we all follow suit? Our hostess spoke English and our host spoke German as their first languages respectively; would one of these be the languages of choice? But then again, the most "obvious" choice would be French since everyone present had some knowledge of the language and we were eating in French-speaking Geneva, right? Wrong. To my pure delight we began a lovely series of anecdotes, stories, and life-histories in (voilà!) English! Well, I thought to myself, poor me, I'll just have to save these other languages for another day. . . . Whew!

In our kitchen layout comes the sometimes necessary role of ingredient substitution, but not in the way it is traditionally conceived. When speaking about raising multilingual children, ingredient substitution comes into play as the sometimes positive relationship between first and second languages. When the foreign language is positively related to the mother tongue, that is, they have the same linguistic roots, then learning is often eased. For example, if you are a native Spanish speaker and you go about learning Italian, you will have a relatively easy time doing this since Spanish and Italian are very similar languages. Let us look at the role of the relationship between first and second languages in more depth now.

THE RELATIONSHIP BETWEEN THE NATIVE AND THE FOREIGN LANGUAGE

Depending on what the relationship is between your child's languages, you could either be faced with a case of "substitution ease"—that is, an easy, logical relationship (Portuguese to French, for example)—or one which requires more creativity to find the patterns and to understand the idiosyncrasies (Arabic to English, for example).

"Easy" vs. "Hard" Foreign Languages

Let us begin at the beginning. When teaching children a foreign language there is something both obvious yet elusive that we should bear in mind. Linguist Steven Pinker of the Massachusetts Institute of Technology writes that to a child, none of the world's estimated 6,000 languages is easier to learn than any other, and children do not favor one language over another. If they did, then only the "easy" languages would survive because no one would bother to tackle the "hard" ones (Pinker 1995). While children cannot actually choose which language environment they are born into, Pinker's point is that no language dies out because children find it too difficult to learn. This makes sense and supports the First Window of Opportunity and the facility children zero to nine months old have at becoming simultaneous, proficient bilinguals, no matter what the language combination. Whether a child learns what his parents might view as an "easy" pair of languages, or one they would label "hard," the child himself is blind to such a judgment.

As adults it is difficult to understand this. We see it differently.

We are fascinated, and often baffled, by aspects of foreign languages such as grammatical gender (how can the moon be feminine in Spanish and masculine in German—and there is no such thing as article gender in English at all) or by the use of adjectives (how can they precede nouns in English—"big *red* house"—follow nouns in French, and be "conjugated" or "declined" in Japanese—"the snow was white" is literally, the "*whited* snow"!). As incredible as it first appears, all children seem to acquire all parts of speech in all languages around the world by the time they are four (Slobin 1992) and write by the age of eight. While normal children may differ in their rate of language development by as much as a year, they all go through the same steps in the same order (babbling in infancy, then single words to simple sentences, then to complex thought expression; recognition of letters, then individual words, then whole sentences, and finally whole books). So when a child is brought up bilingual from birth, she does not judge either of her languages to be "easier" than the other. This changes when a child learns languages after the First Window.

Assuming a child is a "late" bilingual, that is, first a monolingual and then learns a second language in school, it is important to consider the influence that the native language has on learning the second language. This is at the heart of determining the Linguistic Relationship between the first and second (or subsequent) languages.

Werner and Kaplan (1963) stated that all learning takes place in the background of earlier knowledge. We use what we already know to learn new things. What does this tell us about little children and foreign languages? It means that they apply what they already know about words to the new language they are undertaking. Is it easier for a French-speaker to learn Portuguese than for an English-speaker to learn Japanese? Do similar grammatical structures facilitate second language learning? A story might help to clarify the questions and hint at the answers. My husband related this incidence while telling me about his intensive Japanese-language course in Tokyo. He was housed with other young diplomats from around the world who were on scholarship to devote a year of their lives to learning spoken and written Japanese. He recounts the strange ease with which a person from Taiwan could pick up a Japanese newspaper and "read" the morning news. As the Japanese *kanji* writing system is based on Chinese characters, enough similarities exist to allow for such a feat. In many ways, the Taiwanese already knew much of the Japanese written language and could focus on the aspects of speaking. Though he could not "read out loud" what was in the newspaper he could interpret the contents in his own language. The native Spanish-speakers, however, faced with no such similarity, found their work "doubled." On top of learning to speak a language which is quite different from Spanish, the written aspect of Japanese posed several challenges. Japanese uses four alphabets (the *romanji* or Roman alphabet with its twenty-six characters, two kinds of *kana*, one mainly just for foreign words, and the other as a syllabary, each forty-eight to fifty-six characters long, and the *kanji*, or pictograph characters, of which approximately 2,000 are needed to be considered "literate"). Needless to say, the Taiwanese had an advantage over the Colombian, the Ecuadorian, and the Peruvian studying there. On the flip side, however, many Spanish-speakers I know can listen to the Italian news on television or radio with near full comprehension, as "it is so similar to Spanish."

"Who," writes Hakuta (1986: 123), "when faced with an unfamiliar language would not make the most of an already familiar language?" By using knowledge of the native language, second language learners would be following a principle of human development. Does this mean that children and their parents abroad who are faced with the dilemma of choosing a school should look at the language similarities before deciding? Most certainly it makes sense to consider all factors, including the similarities of the native and second languages. Along with the child's age (Window of Opportunity), aptitude (or lack thereof) for languages, personal motivation, and the other ingredients in our Recipe, the relationship between the native and second languages should carry weight in the decision.

When my daughter Natalie came home from school at the beginning of her kindergarten year at the German School with a note saying that French classes were being offered to the students, we considered many points. First of all, at five-and-a-half she was at a perfect age for another language (the Second Window of Opportunity). She has a very high aptitude for languages, as is apparent from her other three languages. She really wanted to take French as many of her friends would be doing it and she said she was "getting behind" the others and was not able to play with the francophones during recess (Motivation). Finally, French is very similar in structure and vocabulary to Spanish, one of her native languages. All ingredients measured up, so we decided to enroll her in the extra classes. She found it to be "easy" and the class so enjoyable that her favorite subject that year was French. Her teacher says she has very good pronunciation (relative to her German-speaking peers). As parents this is something that we will have to continually monitor, but for the present it seems like the relationship between French and Spanish made learning this new language a relatively easy process. This leads to another very intriguing question: Is it true that the more languages you know, the easier it gets to add an additional one? A study conducted by McLaughlin and Nation (1986) sheds light on this very question.

McLaughlin and Nation compared multilingual, bilingual, and monolingual subjects on their ability to learn a "new" linguistic system. The subjects were given "a limited subset of permissible strings from finite-state Markov grammar," or in other words, small writing samples from an unknown language. In some cases they were told the strings or language bits and phrases were rule-based, which implies explicit learning. In other cases the subjects were given the strings without instruction to learn them, which would imply implicit learning. Interestingly enough, multilinguals were found to learn the grammar much better than their bilingual and monolingual counterparts in implicit learning, which Nation and McLaughlin argue was the result of better automated letter- and pattern-recognition skills. "In general, it may be that individuals with more language learning experience build up basic skills that transfer to new situations," says McLaughlin (1990:169). Such evidence has its logic: if a child has already mastered two languages, he may have a certain confidence about embarking on a third or fourth. Why not? If learning languages can be compared to learning an activity in the field of physical activity, then we can see this a little more clearly. If the child can ride a bike, which is different from learning how to roller-skate, which is different from dancing, but which are all within the child's grasp in the kinesthetic realm of learning, then the idea of pursuing a third or fourth language should not seem beyond the grasp of a child who already knows two languages well.

Figure 5.1
Language Sub-Families

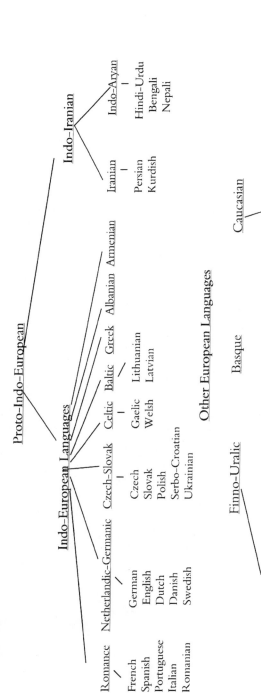

• This is a small sampling of the world's estimated 3,900-6,000 languages.

• According to *Encarta 1996*, the twelve most widely spoken languages with approximate number of native speakers are: 1) Mandarin Chinese 836 million; 2) Hindi 333 mil.; 3) Spanish 332 mil.; 4) English 322 mil.★; 5) Bengali 189 mil.; 6) Arabic 186 mil.; 7) Russian 170 mil.; 8) Portuguese 170 mil.; 9) Japanese 125 mil.; 10) German 98 mil.; 11) French 72 mil.; 12) Malay 50 mil.

★ Adding non-native speakers, English is estimated by the *Guiness Book of World Records 1999* to have 1 billion speakers.

Figure 5.1 (continued)

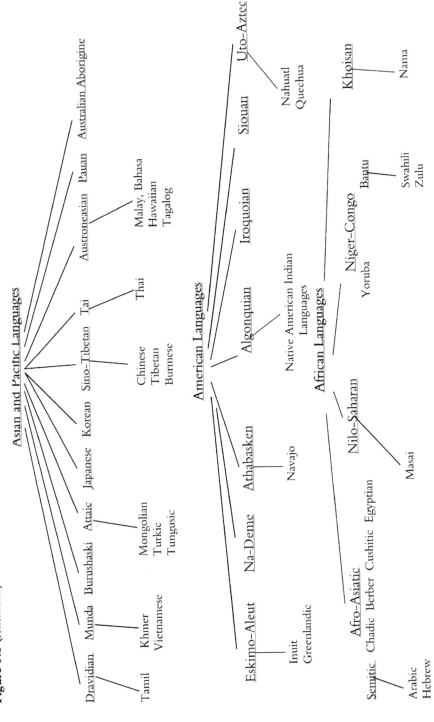

A RECIPE SNAPSHOT ABOUT LANGUAGE RELATIONSHIPS

The Boy Whose Last Name Was Poured Out of a Can of Alphabet Soup: A Polish-German Immigrant in Switzerland

Peter's (whose real name is quite complicated) mother is originally from Poland from an area that was heavily dominated by the Germans during the Second World War. Her parents spoke German and she "picked it up" though not in a formal setting. She is a polyglot (Polish, German, English, French, some Italian, and some Spanish), but she speaks to her son exclusively in Polish. Peter's three strong language influences come from his maternal grandmother who also speaks to him in Polish, from his German father who speaks in a mixture of German and French, and from his school, which is conducted in German. While the mother recognizes that she herself has a talent for languages, she is not yet convinced that Peter shares this. At five years old he still mixes Polish and German to a small extent, though after a short time in a "pure" environment he clarifies which language should be spoken depending on who is present. The mother felt that he would be more "comfortable" in the German school rather than the Swiss (French) system as he spoke French within the school due to friends and because of his environment.

Peter was monolingual in Polish with a passive knowledge of German and French until the Second Window when he began school in German. Polish is from the West Slovak sub-family of languages, distinct from German and differing in many linguistic aspects. French is a Latin-based language not related at all to German or Polish. The mother's idea that attending a German school would be easier than attending a French school was probably based on her successful childhood experiences related to languages. As Peter does not appear to share her gift for languages it is possible that this has contributed to the slowness with which he has begun to communicate in German. The fact that his parents speak French, a Romance language, amongst themselves must add to his confusion. School (always and only in German) should help sort him out while he is still in the Second Window, however, bringing his German skills on par with his Polish. Peter's language task has been complicated by the fact that Polish, German, and French come from three distinct sub-families linguistically (see Figure 5.1). Peter is an only child and both parents work. Having no siblings may have had an influence on his language development.

Each child is unique, whether an only child, an eldest child, a "sandwich," or the tenth of ten. And children within the same family differ in their exact language abilities and their approaches to the task of learning a new language, which leads us to the next area, which is the consideration of siblings.

THE ROLE OF SIBLINGS IN LANGUAGE ACQUISITION

While first-born children usually start speaking earlier than subsequent children, girls generally speak earlier than boys, and monolinguals generally speak slightly earlier than bilinguals, all end up "even" by grade school. Are there benefits to having siblings when trying to learn a new language? Yes and no.

If a child is lucky enough to have a sibling he is generally, but not always, rewarded in the area of language development. One main reason has to do with the amount of exposure they have to words. Sandra Blakeslee of the *International Herald Tribune* writes that "the number of words an infant hears each day is the single most important predictor of later intelligence, school success and social competence" (April 18, 1997). Blakeslee writes about Betty Hart of the University of Kansas in Lawrence and her colleague Todd Ridley of the University of Alaska who studied forty-two children born to professional, working-class, or welfare parents. During the first two-and-a-half years of the children's lives, the scientists spent an hour each month recording every spoken word and every parent-child interaction. They found that professional parents spoke approximately 2,100 words an hour to their children, working-class parents approximately 1,200, and welfare parents just 600. In this spiral effect, parents with high levels of education spoke more to their children. These children, in turn, go on to higher levels of education themselves.

Infants who have older siblings are treated to an increased number of verbal exchanges. I told our pediatrician in Boston I felt I was short-changing our third child because we never had time together alone. All the early stimulation exercises had to be done with the sometimes not-so-helpful involvement of the children who loved to tickle and gurgle at him. She laughed and said there was no better stimulation in the world for a baby than siblings. When we moved to Ecuador shortly after our youngest was three months old, I told our pediatrician in Quito something similar and he said, "The best gift you can give your child is a brother or sister, they all benefit." I am now convinced those doctors knew what they were talking about as I see our youngest flourishing in all areas, especially with language.

In addition to word exchange, there is also play between siblings, and with play comes learning correct social interaction and verbal cues. When my three sit down to eat, it is usually Mateo, the youngest, who raises his glass and says, "*Salúd!*" as if toasting. He learned this from his older brother, who got it from his older sister who in turn mimicked her parents at birthday dinners and other celebrations. The three of them continue such exchanges through the course of the meal which aids all of them in language skills and "proper" social interaction.

The Negative Side of Sibling Intervention

There is a downside to siblings and language development which I observed with my middle child. Having our daughter first was in many ways a blessing; she has a natural maternal instinct for her younger brothers and this has been a great help in many ways. Thankfully, due to this sense of responsibility towards her brothers and her personality as a whole, Natalie never showed signs of jealousy towards them. She loves to please others. But her desire to be helpful passed unintentionally into her brother's language development. When Gabriel, who is two-and-a-half years younger than Natalie, began to talk, she began her job as "official translator." Every need was interpreted, every grunt understood. And she took the initiative to start speaking with her brothers in English and in English only. This further limited the amount of Spanish the children heard daily. I realize I am very lucky that my children like one another and want to help one another, and that they speak to each other at all. However, I cannot help but feel that Natalie's fast-paced, chatty, social character took over some of Gabriel's thinking time, especially in the earlier years. However, at three-years-four-months, he began to tell her to "be quiet, it's my turn!," but did he miss out on a crucial chance to speak more when he was little? I suppose we'll never know, but if I had it to do all over again I probably would manage turn-taking in conversations with more care. Could I have increased his speaking by limiting his sister's conversation? Perhaps. No one can say for sure as other factors could be equally culpable. This leads us to the next chapter, the *Plumbing and Electricity* in our kitchen, which describes the difference in brain structure.

ᡦ

———————— *Chapter 6* ————————

Plumbing and Electricity: The Multilingual Brain

A COOKBOOK WRITTEN BY A PHYSICIST?

I once heard about a cookbook that had been written by a physicist. While he may not have had the greatest sense of taste, he had an exceptional sense of timing. He laid out entire menus based on the exact moment each ingredient of each course had to be added in order for everything to come out hot at the precise moment. The entrée was hot, the soufflé was hot, the wine was chilled, the salad crisp. Great concept, eh? Now that is putting science to good use!

For those parents who are curious about the science in the art of raising multilingual children, I have written the following section which explains the neurological, linguistic, psychological, and pedagogical foundations of my theory. I have tried to give an accurate explanation without being too "thick" in terminology. I hope you find it appetizing.

THE POSSIBLE ROLE OF GENDER IN LANGUAGE ACQUISITION

When my second child, Gabriel, showed signs of being slower than his sister had been at similar stages of language development I began scouring my shelf of baby books for the answer. Why had Natalie a repertoire of 109 words in constant use at twenty-two months and Gabriel only a few dozen? Why did he refuse to speak in Spanish at all and only use English? As related earlier, I brought these concerns to the doctors and they all put a big stop sign up to my complaints and comparisons, which I have since learned were of no help themselves. Never compare children in front of a pediatrician, or in front of the children themselves, I have since learned my lesson. Doctors have seen so many cases, so many "norms" and so many exceptions to the rules, that they see absolutely nothing wrong with a brother and sister being like black and white. Even though they may have been born into the same family with the same parents, they are individuals, with their own set of genes, their own abilities and lack of abilities, and their own life experiences which shape their personalities. And after all, they said, *he's a boy.*

Study after study has shown that boys begin speaking later than girls on the average and are less verbal throughout their lives than their female counterparts. The fact that Gabriel spoke less than his older sister was a "given" in the doctors' eyes. What does this tell us about gauging our expectations when teaching a second language to boys versus girls? Basically, to give it time. As mentioned earlier, even though boys begin speaking later than girls, they catch up in terms of vocabulary, syntax, and grammar by grade school, but males will be less verbal overall throughout their lives.

And boys and girls seem to use their brains differently when using languages. As mentioned earlier, if you are right-handed and left-hemisphere dominant (male or female), you have your language center located in your left frontal and parietal lobes. An interesting study related by Christine Gorman (1995) showed that while men "compartmentalize language into the left hemisphere, recent MRI (magnetic resonance imaging) scans show that women use both hemispheres in processing verbal exchange." The images of the MRI show how the left-hemisphere language area of men "lit up" when responding to a question, but only in a very small and delineated area. The scans of the women showed how both left and right hemispheres react when answering a question. Why is this? Other studies have indicated that women "take in" more information when communicating, such as facial expression, body language, and tone of voice (located in the right hemisphere) whereas men focus mainly on the content of what is being said (left hemisphere). There are benefits to both systems, say researchers. Perhaps men are better able to concentrate on the detail and exactness of responding to what is said with a minimal of words, while women have a better overall sense of the entire message that is communicated and the feeling behind it. Still other studies have measured the number of words and utterances made by small children (three- to five-year-olds) at play. It was found that the little girls narrated their way through their activity and spoke nearly the entire time. Boys spoke sixty percent less than the girls, and forty to fifty percent of what they *did* utter were non-words (animal noises, car horns, train's whistles, etc.). These few examples are meant to open the reader to the idea that males and females approach language from different angles (or at least different sides of the brain) and perhaps approach foreign languages from different perspectives as well. This right-versus-left hemisphere information leads us to another area where some language learners differ from others, and that is hand use.

THE POSSIBLE ROLE OF HAND USE IN LANGUAGE LEARNING

This last area has yet to be proven, but it is worth considering as evidence is building up in its favor daily. Hand use generally reflects either right or left hemisphere dominance. Most right-handed people are left-hemisphere dominant (ninety-five percent) and have their main language center located in the left frontal and parietal lobes. About thirty percent of the left-handed people in the world are right-hemisphere dominant or double-dominant, meaning they use their hemispheres equally, and seventy percent are left-hemisphere dominant, just like right-handed people (Springer and Deutsch 1989; Restak 1984; Mai 1998).

The brain looks very much like a walnut, divided down the middle by a band of fibers. The two sides of the brain, the left hemisphere and the right hemisphere, work as a single unit, but "specialize" in their functions. In general, for the majority of the world's population the left hemisphere is the seat of logical thinking, reasoning, and language abilities. The right hemisphere houses visio-spatial ability, music, and general creativity.

Research on multilinguals shows that those who speak more than one language depend on their right hemispheres more for language processing. Would enhancing the right hemisphere by learning a second language have any influence over other right-hemisphere functions?

Left	Right
• Spoken Language	• Body Language
• Written Language	• Interpreting Facial Expressions
• Logical/Reasoning Skills	• Spatial Skills (puzzles, manipulation
• Mathematics/Number Skills	of geometric figures, patterns,
• Scientific Skills	figures)
• Reasoning	• Music (singing)
• Music (composition)	• Art
	• Insight
	• Imagination

In the majority of normal subjects, the rules of *semantics* (the actual structure of a proper sentence) are normally located in the left hemisphere, and *prosody* (the emotional tone related to the sentence) is in the right hemisphere. One loses the ability to speak in a proper sentence (word order, choice of vocabulary, appropriate pronunciation) when there is a stroke in the left hemisphere. One loses the ability to inflect intonation and to gauge the different voices (irony, sarcasm, disbelief, anger) when there is a stroke in the right hemisphere. Could this mean that healthy bilinguals have the possibility of increased prosody because of increased use of the right-hemisphere language area? It's an interesting prospect. Are there other right-hemisphere related abilities that show increased activity due to multilingualism?

Creativity and Multilinguals

Research on bilingualism and divergent thinking undertaken in Canada, the United States, Ireland, Mexico, and Singapore all show that those people with more languages were more creative in their problem solving. L. A. Ricciardelli proposed this creativity–language link and cites numerous cases supporting her hypothesis as well (Ricciardelli 1992). It would seem logical, however, to suppose that if the right hemisphere houses creativity and if multilinguals use their right hemisphere more, then multilinguals should be more creative. Bilinguals were shown to be more "flexible" in their thinking and showed more "originality" in their interpretations.

Natasha Lvovich writes in her book *The Multilingual Self*, about her own increased *synesthesia*—the capacity to recall words by "thinking of their colors or imagining them pending in the air, while examining their shape, smoothness, position in space, or feel at touch" (1997:14). An example would be how Lvovich assigns colors and shapes to the days of the week: "In French, *Lundi* is pale wax pink; in Russian, *Ponedel'nik* is grayish and dull; and Monday is in orange-red-brown gamma" (12). Are multilinguals better at this type of imaging? Is this type of mnemonic device a "natural" one for multilinguals? Or is the ability to distinguish similar labels (Monday=*Lundi*=*Ponedel'nik*) a necessity in the multilingual's mind, who will therefore use color or texture or form as aids in distinguishing them?

Another right-hemisphere strength is in spatial ability. Research has shown that polyglots are better at visual puzzles. They can see the two faces kissing each other in the picture of two vases. They are better at seeing the image of an old woman etched into the collar of the young woman. They can envision the movement of shapes in space and can tell if one shape can be successfully superimposed onto another. Does this necessarily mean that multilingualism and spatial skills go hand in hand? Or does it mean that enhancing one enhances the other?

Another right-hemisphere language job has to do with facial expression and body language. Are multilinguals more adept at interpreting facial expressions? And if they are, is this because when learning another language one has the tendency to use all clues available, including facial expression and gestures to successfully decipher a new language? Or because the right hemisphere has been stimulated via the second language learning experience and therefore facial expression recognition is enhanced? These questions percolate into the emerging field of creativity and multilingualism, which is in its infant stage, but which promises to yield fascinating insights in the near future. While it is now generally accepted that multilinguals are probably using *more* of their brain than their monolingual counterparts, it also is tempting to state that by learning multiple languages children are probably enhancing their ability to be creative in at least the areas of facial expression interpretation, spatial puzzle solving, and synesthesia, but the final say on this rests with research yet to be undertaken. Suffice it to say for now that the benefits of multilingualism are fast growing with each new study undertaken.

Are there any noticeable differences in how right- and left-handed people learn second languages? Not that I know of, but the questions it leaves relate to the structure of the brain, and with a change in structure can come a change in where second language is localized. A trained eye can tell what sex and which handed a person is by looking at his or her brain. Both hand use and the sex of a person change the size and, to a certain extent, shape of important areas in the brain, thereby making it easy for the trained eye to know something about the person by just looking at his or her exposed brain. The question of hemisphere dominance is important to our discussion about how children learn languages because it may help us guess why some children have an easier time acquiring languages than others. Somewhere between eight and a half and ten and a half percent of the world's population is left-handed. Many of these people have their primary language areas located in their right hemispheres or are double-hemisphere dominant. Does this population learn languages differently? Is there a relationship between this approximately ten percent of the population and those who have a higher aptitude for languages? We do not know, though it would be a convenient correlation. I find this personally intriguing as my high-aptitude, left-handed daughter, who is extremely right-hemisphere oriented, always amazes me when it comes to both language and creativity. Such an idea is like the lingering of the smell of a chocolate cake just baked when you have an empty stomach, you wish to pursue it blindly, though you know it may not be good for you. For now, suffice it to say that most right-handed people house their second languages in the right hemisphere, but it's a mixed bag when we look at left-handed people (see Figure 6.1). Is one group better at foreign languages than the other? No one knows for sure. Is there a relationship between aptitude and hemisphere dominance? We do not know that with certainty either. These are ideas, however, that are worth following in the coming years as more and more research is conducted in this area.

Now we turn to an overview of the Multilingual Brain.

THE MULTILINGUAL BRAIN

As we saw in the previous section, it would be nice to say that there is "the" right way to go about aiding children with multilingual skills, but each family must assess itself individually to see how each "ingredient" is measured in its own case. One thing that can be said about

Figure 6.1
Right- vs. Left-Handed People

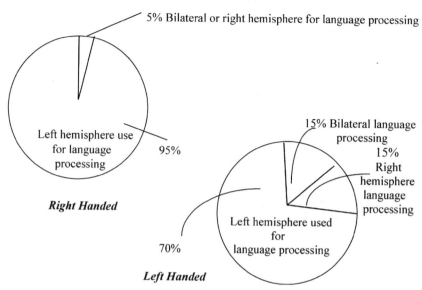

all cases, however, is that your child's age is an influencing factor on exactly how he goes about learning the language. We turn to the neurological foundations for this assertion next.

It was once believed that if children were exposed to a second language before their teenage years (Penfield and Roberts 1959), they would become fluent. So many exceptions cropped up that the age was dropped to two (Lennenberg 1967). Now some present-day neurologists proclaim that the real limit is just seven to nine months old (Werker 1997). How could all of these ages truly be the "cut-off" for language learning? I believe that a good part of the answer uniting these previous researchers' work lies in the Windows of Opportunity that the brain offers us when learning a foreign language. There are different ages when the brain is better prepared to receive a foreign language successfully.

THE BRAIN AND MULTILINGUAL CHILDREN

To balance the enthusiasm I have for this subject, it is only fair to begin with a cautionary note. Dr. Mark Greenberg (1997) of Harvard University posed a very intriguing question: If faces are different, why not brain structure? Even though each of us has two eyes and two ears, a nose and a mouth, our faces look different. So why not our brains? And as each person's face differs from another's, there are even subtler differences in the two halves of the same face of each individual. If you draw a line down the middle of your nose and look carefully you will see that the halves are not mirror images of one another (that's why we have a "good" side). This leads us to wonder about the "hard facts" we base our knowledge of the brain on. As most of the evidence found in this area is based on right-handed male stroke victims, a good number of people do not match the cases presented. This includes young children, both monolingual and multilingual. The factors of age, gender, and even handedness—which reflects hemispherical dominance in the brain and the language center location in most cases—challenge our ability to generalize here.

While most of the world *is* right handed (eighty-nine to ninety-three percent worldwide), only forty-nine percent are males. Most stroke victims who make up the body of evidence are monolingual adult males. Young, left-handed females, like my daughter, for example, may or may not have language located in the same areas as the research here indicates. In all likelihood the similarities are greater than the subtle differences (like the noses on our face which *do* the same thing, they just look a bit different from our neighbor's), so it makes sense to look further into what is known to date about cerebral structure. Warnings aside, now let's look at the brain and language functioning in multilinguals as a whole.

Nature and Nurture in Language Development

Each child is born with a set number of neurons (some 100 billion) which correspond to him through genetics; basically, he gets what his parents give him (Restak 1984; Mai 1998). What he does with those neurons is the nurture part of this biological-environmental soup. The connections made between these cells (neurons), or the *synapses* that are formed, are contingent on a child's experience with the world.

Imagine all the individual cells that make up your child's brain, kind of like looking up at the sky on a clear fall night and seeing an endless number of stars. Now try to imagine a line from one cell to another, or from one star to another. These connections between cells (stars) are the synapses, and depending on how many synapses are formed, you are able to learn and remember things. Some fifty trillion synapses are formed at birth, climbing to 1,000 trillion in the first few months of life. How does this increase happen so quickly? Every little life experience forms a connection, or reinforces an already existing one. When Johnny sees a cat, for example, and we call it "cat," a connection (synapse), or rather several connections, are made. Why several? Because synapses are created at the visual stimulus of the cat itself, the auditory stimulus of the word "cat," the sound "meow," the fact that it has soft fur, the fact that it goes in the category of other four-legged animals, and that it likes to chase birds and eat fish, all form various connections in the brain. In a similar fashion language connections, or synapses, are made.

By the time a child is nine months old, the production of longer-distance connections which are not just synaptic (single cell to single cell), but rather groups of cells to groups of cells are formed. Instead of a bunch of loose cells with connections to other loose cells, we now have connections between groups of cells which specialize in particular areas (brain cells for physical movement, brain cells for emotion, brain cells for music). These longer distance connections are what creates what is known as *myelin insulation* in the brain, which in great part determines the speed with which information is carried. The stronger the connections, the greater the myelin insulation, the faster one is able to retrieve information stored in the brain.

Many good teachers have probably already told you that the greater number of ways you put information into your head, the easier it will be to retrieve. If you learn of the cat as an animal, as a creature that says meow, as being four-legged with claws, as having soft fur, etc., you are more likely to recall what it is the next time you see it, than if you only learn it in a single way (pointing to a picture of a cat in a book and labeling it "cat," for example). This is true of any type of learning. This is why teaching a child a word in a foreign language by simply translating it is not nearly as effective as having the child relate the word to a loving caregiver (emotional attachment), saying the word out loud (verbal, muscular), having him act out a scene in a play using the word (kinesthetic, imaginative), writing the word (motor coordination), reading the word (visual), painting the meaning of the word (creative), or using the word in a song (musical), or in imaginative play. Each of these activities helps put "cat" into a greater number of "categories" in the brain so when we look for "cat" the next time, our odds of finding it fast are improved. It is as if I really need to be able to find my blue socks in the morning. If I put a pair of blue socks in *each* of my dresser drawers the night before, I do not have to go to precisely the "right" drawer, as blue socks are stored in all of them, making my search easier. If a language is learned in a variety of ways, we are more likely to remember it than if a single method is used.

A BRIEF HISTORY OF THE BRAIN AND POLYGLOTS

It is fascinating to note that most of what is known to date about the brain has occurred in just the past few decades. While the brain has been of interest to philosophers and physicians for thousands of years, the tools to measure brain activity were fairly limited until the later half of this century.

As early as the second century A.D. there were attempts to understand this complex organ, but progress was slow-going (see Figure 6.2). Information about brain structure remained pretty stagnant until the 1600s when a general outline of the brain's function was gleaned by studying brains exposed after death. In 1664 Thomas Willis published *Anatomy of the Brain* which was illustrated by the architect Sir Christopher Wren, bringing the intricate details of brain structure to the common man. But knowledge of the exact work of the brain was still a mystery. Franz Joseph Gall ventured that the bumps, balls, and indentations found on each person's skull could explain their mental strengths and weaknesses in his "science" of phrenology. But it was not until the early 1820s that knowledge of electrical impulses in the brain and their relationship to their areas of activity were measured by the first galvanometer (which preceded today's EEG, or electroencephalogram). In the early 1900s the smallest unit of the brain, the neuron, and the connections between neurons was brought to light by Santiago Ramon y Cajál. This indicated to the world that it was not the size of the brain (nor the bumps and lumps on the skull) that indicated learning had taken place, but rather the number of connections made between parts of the brain which mattered. After all, upon death it was discovered that Einstein's brain was actually smaller than average for a man his size, showing that size alone was not what strengthened connections between groups of neurons. Einstein, however, made more connections than the average man between the neurons in his brain. His brain showed us that what is of much greater

Figure 6.2
A Brief History of the Brain and Polyglots (Tokuhama-Espinosa)

2nd century A.D.	Galen, Greek physician who learned about brain structure by dissecting farm animals and apes.
1600s	General outline of brain organization gleaned from brains exposed after death.
1664	Thomas Willis published *Cerebri Anatome* (Anatomy of the Brain), illustrated by Sir Christopher Wren.
1780s	Franz Josef Gall--phrenology
1820s	First galvanometer, predecessor of the EEG
1890-1906	Santiago Ramon y Cajál--Identified the neuron as individual and the "gaps" between them were labeled synapses. William James, Father of Psychology.
1930s and 1940s	Brain as a "telephone switchboard."
1940s and 1950s	Wilder Penfield, electrical stimulation of patients undergoing neurosurgery.
1960	Alexandre Luria (memory), Roger W. Sperry, Michael S. Gazzaniga (corpus callosum).
1976	Dr. H.H. Kornhuber recorded EEG (electroencephalogram) signals from healthy volunteers.
1980s	Brain as a "computer." CAT scan (Computerized Axial Tomography) – stationary brain, good for locating tumors, etc. PET scans (positron emission tomography)-- Measures brain activity Spin-offs of EEG: BEAM (Brain Electrical Activity Mapping)-- Color images of electrical movement SPM (Significance Probability Mapping)-- locate exact point of origin
1990s	Improvements on imaging (three dimensional, real-time and emphasis on healthy subjects).

Current Brain Facts (Mai 1998):
□ There are between 10-100 billion neurons.
□ Connections between these neurons are electrical and chemical.
□ Each of the neurons may have over a thousand synapses (points of contact between nerve cells), meaning there are between 10 trillion-100 trillion synapses in the brain.

importance than size were the number of folds and "gray matter" created by connections between neurons.

In the 1940s and 1950s we began to get a glimpse of how different areas of the brain related to different memories and skills with Penfield's electrical stimulation of brains of conscious patients undergoing surgery. By placing an electrode on one part of the brain, it was found that the patient recalled the peculiar odors of his childhood kitchen. When placed in another area the patient would remember the exact words of a conversation that had taken place several years earlier. Such demonstrations gave backing to the hunch that nothing is ever forgotten, it is all a question of how easy memories are to retrieve (Penfield 1959).

By the 1960s work began on "mapping" the brain in earnest. But the more work that was undertaken, the more complex a task seemed to emerge. Differences between left-hemisphere dominant people and right-hemisphere dominant people became more evident. The role of the once little-acknowledged right hemisphere became glamorized. Learning to think "from the right-side of the brain" came into vogue in the 1980s and remains so even today. It wasn't until the late 1970s and the early 1980s, however, that researchers had the tools to begin studying the brains of healthy people. Up until this point much of the information gleaned about the brain had come either from stroke victims or from unfortunate patients undergoing surgery for ailments such as epilepsy. But in 1976, Dr. H. H. Kornhuber, a German neurophysiologist, recorded EEG readings from healthy volunteers (Restak 1984: 83–84), setting the stage for a completely new era of brain research.

Since the 1980s the common use of such machines, which can evaluate the human brain in a variety of ways, has contributed to our ongoing accumulation of knowledge. The CAT scan (Computerized Axial Tomography) was introduced at this time, which provided excellent imaging of stationary brains, helping to localize tumors, for example. PET scans (Positron Emission Tomography), on the other hand, measure brain activity, so brains could be observed while completing a designated task.

Two spin-offs of the EEG included the BEAM (Brain Electrical Activity Mapping) which provided color images of electrical movement and the SPM (Significance Probability Mapping) which could locate the exact point of origin of the electrical firing of neurons. These two machines made it possible to identify with greater accuracy which part of the brain was functioning with which task. In the 1990s there were great improvements in the quality of the images that these machines could create (three-dimensional, real-time, and emphasis on healthy subjects), meaning that not only was accuracy improving, but so was imaging.

PAST AND PRESENT BELIEFS ABOUT THE MULTILINGUAL BRAIN

As measurement of the mental processes associated with language acquisition has grown, progress in another field has given rise to increased interest in multilinguals. In the post–World War II era it was not very typical for families to be relocated overseas, for diplomatic missions to be in so many different nations, or for multiple languages as a whole to be of such central importance in so many people's lives. With present-day global needs, however, research about multilinguals is on the rise.

Comments regarding multilinguals and their brains were sparse in the medical community until the 1950s. One of the first publications to focus on the multilingual brain came from W. Penfield and L. Roberts in 1959. They stated in *Speech and Brain Mechanisms* that until "nine to twelve" a child can learn "two or three languages as easily as one." In 1967 E. Lennenberg wrote in *Biological Foundations of Language* that there was "a biologically based critical period" for learning a second language "between two and about 13," years of age.

It wasn't until the late 1970s, however, that actual experiments were carried out and empirical findings were documented related to multilinguals' brains. Exciting research in 1978 by George Ojemann and Harry Whitaker was conducted around a "Theory of Separate Representation" which they reported in *The Bilingual Brain*, in the *Archives of Neurology, 35*. This work stated that there were actually different areas of the brain responsible for different languages, but which had a point of overlap. M. L. Albert and L. Obler expanded on this "Dual System Hypothesis" in *The Bilingual Brain: Neuropsychological and Neurolinguistic Aspects of Bilingualism*, a year later. Loraine Obler introduced the emerging importance of *"Right hemisphere participation in second language acquisition"* (Albert and Olber 1979). Here she wrote that the right hemisphere actually plays a much larger role in language acquisition than was ever thought of before. When a stroke occurred in a subject's right hemisphere, bilinguals were far more likely to suffer language loss than monolinguals. Fred Genesee and his colleagues showed similar findings in their experiments in 1978 as well.

In 1980 Linda Galloway contributed a fascinating case study to Paradis' work (Paradis 1983) regarding a heptaglot who suffered from aphasia after a stroke. Her work confirmed that languages learned at different points in a person's life were located in different areas of the brain. Michel Paradis himself documented all known cases of polyglot aphasia from 1843 to the early 1980s and verified that language loss differed depending on when the language was learned.

The most current research in the field of neurology and linguistics brings us further evidence that children may be born with an innate capacity to learn any number of languages, but this diminishes over time. As mentioned when we first introduced the First Window of Opportunity, in 1997 Janet Werker identified key times when children are able to discriminate "foreign" sounds and showed how this ability is lost over time. Lila Gleitman and Elissa Newport refined our knowledge of "milestones of normal language development" which defined the parameters of language capacity in children (1995). In 1997 John H. Schumann showed neurologically how emotional memory affects second language learning in *The Neurobiology of Affect in Language*. This additional element has brought our present knowledge of how languages are learned and what areas of the brain are involved to a new height.

BRAIN STRUCTURE IN ALL THREE WINDOWS OF OPPORTUNITY

There are seven primary areas of the brain related to language production and reception in monolinguals, and two additional areas related to the motivation or affect of second language development. These nine areas of the brain reflect what is known to date about language production, reception, and usage by multilinguals. As parents of multilingual children, how can this information serve us?

Knowing that there are different areas of the brain related to speaking, listening, reading, and writing allows us to sympathize with the complications of attaining multilingualism and gives us an understanding as to why some children achieve verbal bilingualism but not literacy skills. Knowing that there are specific areas of the brain related to motivation and that they can be effected both positively and negatively also guides us. Understanding that motivation is an area we can influence by the types of experiences we afford our children in the home gives us some control over the language acquisition process.

What Monolingual Stroke Victims Can Teach Us

Before 1978, neurologists had not studied a healthy bilingual brain. Before this point all of the information we had about the brain came from stroke patients with "damaged" brains, or those undergoing surgery for epilepsy. What these unfortunate cases taught the world, however, was invaluable as different types of language loss could be documented.

Howard Gardner in *The Shattered Mind* (1975) listed various types of aphasia, or language loss, which was caused by strokes in victims he observed at the Aphasia Research Center of the Boston Administration's Medical Hospital. Over ninety-five percent of the cases of aphasia occurred in patients with damage to the left hemisphere (Geschwind 1997). "The varieties of aphasia form a fascinating class of disorders," though it is often tragic to see their suffering, writes Gardner (1975:28). Paraphrasing Gardner, and according to his observations, stroke victims can be grouped into those that:

1. understand reasonably well, yet can only speak in short, elliptical phrases devoid of the "little" parts of speech;
2. have only minimal understanding yet can talk in great length in a syntactically rich but often meaningless jargon;
3. repeat everything without understanding what they say;
4. are proficient in all language function but repetition;
5. suffer from "pure alexia" injury to the posterior regions of the brain, meaning the victim is unable to read printed matter, while visual perception is normal for everything except words. Strangely enough, someone with this aphasia can write, but not read his own writing (Gardner 1975: 16).

Add to these five areas (as defined by the five aphasia-types above) two others related to language processing: the auditory cortex (6) for listening ability, and an additional area related to reading (7) which came to light in cases of Japanese stroke victims. This additional reading area distinguishes the difference between the Roman alphabet languages and pictographs. Sumiko Sasanuma (1975:369–383) showed that in Japanese patients, left hemisphere damages resulted in the loss of *kana* which parallels the English Roman alphabet. Similar left hemisphere damage in English-speakers led to the inability to read. But as *kanji* are visually dependent *and* have several sounds which can be used for the same character depending on the context, *right* hemisphere damage can lead to its loss in Japanese language speakers. Thus, writing systems based on pictographs as found in Chinese or Japanese are found in a different area of the brain.

THE AREAS OF THE BRAIN USED FOR LANGUAGE

In total then, seven areas of the brain can be said to participate in language processing in monolinguals around the world. These seven areas are roughly the same as identified over 100 years ago by Carl Wernicke (1874). They are detailed in Harvard University Neurobiologist Norman Geschwind's paper on "Specializations of the Human Brain." The following is a rough summary of the same.

Speaking, Hearing, Reading, and Writing in the Brain

Speaking

The underlying structure of speech arises in *Wernicke's area* (in the left temporal lobe). It is then transferred through the *arcuate fasciculus* (a band of fibers connecting Wernicke's and Broca's areas) to *Broca's area* (in the left frontal lobe), where it sends signals to the adjacent face muscles of the mouth, the lips, the tongue, the larynx, and other muscles, creating the spoken word.

Hearing

First the sounds used to form a word are initially heard in the *primary auditory cortex* (in the temporal lobe); the signal passes through the adjacent *Wernicke's area* and is "decoded" as a verbal message.

Reading

When a word is read, the visual pattern from the *primary visual cortex* (in the occipital lobe) is transmitted to the *angular gyrus* (which probably mediates between the visual and auditory centers of the brain), and then causes a transformation which elicits the auditory form of the word in *Wernicke's area*.

Writing

Writing a word in response to an oral instruction requires information to be passed along the same pathways as reading, but in the opposite direction: from the *auditory cortex* to *Wernicke's area* to the *angular gyrus*. The actual writing is a function of the *motor cortex*. This leads us to an interesting question: If the complexities of the brain require all of this just to speak and write one language, what about bilingual or multilingual individuals? Does the bilingual utilize twice the "brain space" to ponder words (spoken and written), or is there a single mental process, regardless of the number of languages? I have often observed polyglots in situations where they seem to effortlessly scan their minds in a single instant for the appropriate word to explain a concept. Does this mean that the areas of the brain are different for each language and there is a simultaneous search in all languages, or are the areas of the brain the same? Another group of stroke patients offers us a clue.

Multilingual Stroke Patients

The stories of bilinguals or multilinguals who lost their languages due to strokes can help us understand the parts of the brain devoted to language production. How bilingual stroke victims recover their languages gives an indication of how multilingual children's brains store their first, second, and successive languages.

Paradis (1983), along with studies by M. L. Albert and L. Obler (1979), found that in about half the cases the bilingual victim's two languages recover at the same rate. The other half were a mixture of those whose first language recovered first, the most recently used language acquired first, or in some rare cases the return of the languages fluctuated. Paradis theorized that this variation in recovery patterns was due to what he labeled the "dual system hypothesis." In this system the two languages are represented in overlapping but distinct areas of the brain. Damage in a stroke victim then, could occur in the area of language A, the area of language B, or their overlapping area, explaining the differences in recovery (see Figure 6.3).

This theory of "separate representation" was first seen in results achieved by George Ojemann and Harry Whitaker (1978) in which they mapped the bilingual-relevant regions of the cortex in two patients (one was a thirty-seven-year-old Dutch male who had learned

Figure 6.3
Language Overlap Hypothesis

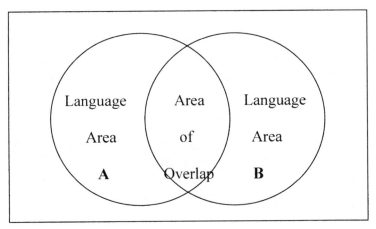

Ojemann and Whitaker's theory of "separate representation" shows that while some parts of the brain are devoted to Language A and some are related just to Language B, these areas overlap in some places.

English at twenty-five, the other was a twenty-year-old American female who spoke Spanish at home) who were undergoing surgery for epilepsy. A mild electrical stimulus was applied and the patients were asked to provide the name of objects in pictures in specific languages. The belief was that the electrical stimulation would inhibit activity where it was applied, leading to an inability to name objects. Their findings confirmed the dual system hypothesis. In their own words:

For both subjects there was an area where stimulation led to inability to name in both languages, but there were also areas that showed reliable tendencies toward inhibition of one or the other of the languages. There was also the suggestion that the weaker language was represented in a wider area of the cortex [right as well as left hemisphere] than the primary language. (Hakuta 1986: 87–88)

This is very consistent with other studies which indicate that people who learn languages after the First Window of Opportunity (zero to nine months old) have their second language spread out to use areas of the right hemisphere not utilized in monolinguals. Paradis writes in the Epilogue to his collection of cases that

[a]ccording to this hypothesis, bilinguals have two subsets of neural connections, one for each language . . . while at the same time they possess one larger set from which they are able to draw elements of either language at any time . . . one has equal access to both languages, though in normal circumstances the search is confined to the lexicon of one language. . . .The ease with which a given item can be retrieved seems to be a function of both the frequency of use and the time elapsed since it was last encountered, be it within one or several languages. (Paradis 1983: 812–813)

In other words, the two languages are separated in the brain, but can be called upon simultaneously for use. While words can be found in either of the two languages at any time, the bilingual usually confines himself to one at a time. The ability to retrieve words and use a language depends on the frequency with which they are used.

Two Additional Areas: The Brain Structure of Motivation

Schumann (1997) writes of two other areas of the brain related to language production in multilinguals. He bases his theory on where "motivation" or "affect" is located cerebrally and then applied this to the language learner. This leads us now from the physical structure of the brain and the areas used in language production to the concept of motivation in second language learning and the physiological base for such a supposition. Assuming motivation is a vital factor in learning a language, where is its place in a multilingual child's brain and how can we stimulate it?

According to Schumann, the *amygdala* and the *frontal lobes* play a significant role in regulating the evaluation of emotion in our brains. Schumann searched to find whether there was some mechanism in the brain that allowed emotion to influence cognition and learning. In 1989 he identified the amygdala, which assesses the motivational significance and emotional relevance of stimuli. Based on the amygdala's appraisals of different situations, the brain allocates attention and memory resources to various problems; the variability in such allocations is what affects learning. In other words, if you are emotionally driven, you will learn. The second area of the brain related to second language motivation is the *neocortex*, or frontal lobes, located just behind your forehead. This is where "higher level" thinking takes place and where decisions are made. Therefore, what you feel is remembered in the amygdala and evaluated in the frontal lobes.

Schumann also notes research from Jacobs and Nadel which points out that while the hippocampus (which is usually associated with memory) does not become fully operational until between the ages of eighteen months to three years, the amygdala, or "emotional memory," functions from early infancy. This is why we can have strong feelings about experiences that we cannot fully recall. Sad examples of this can be found in infants who are abused and then removed from the abusive environment. In later childhood they have no memory of the abuse, but still suffer emotionally and psychologically. Therefore, an event may be "recorded as an unconscious emotional memory in the amygdala and related areas" and can affect the individual's behavior later in life (Schumann 1997: 44). What does this mean for multilingual children?

When we decide that something is good, pleasant, agreeable, horrid, fearsome, or disgusting, such experiences are remembered in the amygdala. These positive and negative experiences are recalled when we have new, similar experiences, and they can influence how we learn things. For example, if we like someone who speaks another language (the neighbor, the teacher, a friend, relative, or caregiver), then we *want* to learn their language. Our experiences with the language are greatly influenced, writes Schumann, by our emotional relation to those languages. This is the basis for adding on these two other areas of the brain in our overall structure of the brain and language in multilinguals.

BRAIN STRUCTURE, LANGUAGE AND MULTILINGUAL CHILDREN

Nine Areas of the Brain Devoted to Language in Multilingual Children

This brings us to a total of nine areas of the brain devoted to language production in multilingual children (see Figure 6.4). In summary, the first seven areas are shared by monolingual and multilinguals alike as language is processed in Wernicke's area and Broca's area, which are connected by the arcuate fasciculus. The motor cortex, audio cortex, and visual cortex aid language in hearing, seeing, and writing. The angular gyrus connects the audio and visual cortex

Figure 6.4
Brain Structure and Language in the Multilingual

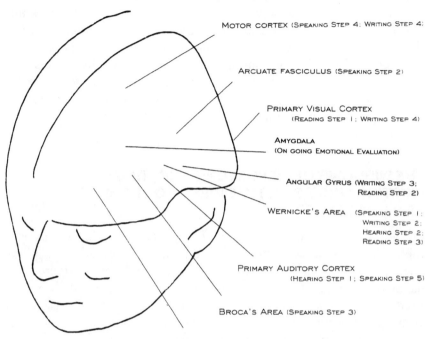

areas of the brain. The last two areas of the amygdala and the frontal lobes are related to our emotional memory with language experiences. These nine areas make up the framework within which children process their multiple languages.

Which Brain Hemisphere Is Dominant in Multilinguals?

Most of the people in the world have language localized in the left parietal and frontal lobes, are right-handed, and left-hemisphere dominant. A bilingual who shows greater right-hemisphere involvement in the processing of language is one who has learned his second language after the First Window of Opportunity, usually many years after. This coincides with the idea that up through the First Window (zero to nine months) all languages are localized in the same spot (left hemisphere) in the brain. After this time, enough neuro-connections are formed to allow for language functions to "specialize"; the native language(s) staying in the left hemisphere, while the newer languages tend to be more spread out or localized in the right. This does not mean to say that all bilinguals are right-hemisphere dominant. On the contrary, as most of the world begins left-hemisphere dominant, they remain so. Cerebral dominance does not change due to this fact.

We now turn to a unification of the many ideas presented so far in this book, joining together the information on the brain with linguistic, psychological, and educational theories of language learning in children.

THE WINDOWS OF OPPORTUNITY: UNITING EXISTING LINGUISTIC THEORIES ABOUT CHILDREN AND LANGUAGES

The *Windows of Opportunity for Foreign Language Acquisition* is a theory harmonious with much of the existing information on bilinguals to date. Several linguists and researchers have considered the factor of timing and age of acquisition in foreign language learning: Fred Genesee et al. (1979), Birgit Harley (1986), Barry McLaughlin (1985a), Catherine Snow and M. Hoefnagel-Höhle (1978), and M. Swain (1981) among them, and their work has helped to shape my own theory. Others such as John Schumann (1997) and Ellen Bialystok (1995) have addressed the factor of motivation and other psychological aspects of language learning. Yet others have done formidable work on the factor of aptitude for foreign language learning, the role of opportunity, and the relationship between first and second languages. Each of these factors is a piece of the puzzle.

Others have done work defining the degrees of success of bilinguals. Jim Cummins (1980), for example, believes that there are three types of bilingualism: limited, partial, and proficient. Those with limited bilingualism have low proficiency in both languages. Those with partial bilingualism have native-like abilities in one of the languages. Those with proficient bilingualism have native-like control in both languages (see Figure 6.5). Cummins believes that "limited bilingualism" results in negative cognitive consequences and that "proficient bilingualism" has positive consequences. I believe that children who learn their languages in the First Window of Opportunity (zero to nine months old) are *always* proficient bilinguals if their parents are consistent in the language strategy they use.

Figure 6.5
Levels of Bilingualism

Cummins	First Language	Second Language
Limited bilingualism	Low proficiency	Low proficiency
Partial bilingualism	Native-like control	Low proficiency
Proficient bilingualism	Native-like control	Native-like control

Similarly, Edith Harding and Philip Riley write of bilingualism as having "degrees" of success from someone who "speaks two languages perfectly" (Bloomfield 1933) to where "the speaker of one language can produce meaningful utterances in another [language]" (Haugen 1972). There is a striking correlation, however, of those who speak "perfectly" to those who learned their languages during the First Window of Opportunity. We turn next to examining how some of these theories fit together to give us a whole picture, with a discussion of some of the choices we will have to make along the way regarding how we bring up multilingual children.

Using Cummins' idea of "limited, partial and proficient bilinguals," Harding and Riley's concept of "bilingualism by degrees" and my own "Windows of Opportunity for Foreign Language Acquisition," I have come up with a possible scenario of how children progress through the different stages of bilingual abilities. In these charts there is a continuum of time on one level (infancy to adulthood), paralleled by an accumulation of language skills (beginning with basic communication and evolving to sophisticated literacy skills) (see Figure 6.6). These language skills are achieved with varying degrees of fluency (limited, then partial, then proficient) by each person. If a child learns his languages in the First Window of Opportunity, I contend that he can become a proficient bilingual by the end of early childhood orally (speaking skills) (see Figure 6.7). That same child can become a proficient bilingual in literacy skills (reading and writing) as early as the end of the Second Window (age eight) or at least before early adolescence.

For example, Alexander's mother has spoken to him in her native English since birth. His father has spoken to him in his native French since birth. Both parents read, sang, and played with him in their

Figure 6.6
Types of Bilinguals

Term Used By	0-3 years	3-11 years	12-19 years	19+ years
Genesee et al. 1978	Early	Late	Late	Late
McLaughlin 1978	Simultaneous	Successive	Successive	Successive
Harding and Riley 1986/96	Infant	Child	Adolescent	Adult

Note that twenty years ago all children under three were categorized together, whereas now the first nine months of life seem to be quite different.

Figure 6.7
The First Window of Opportunity

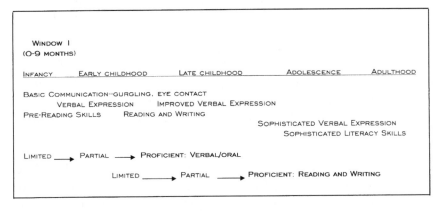

own language. As Alex grew, he progressed through the stages of having limited speaking abilities in his languages in early childhood (similar to any monolingual his age). He then gained partial fluency around three-and-a-half years old, after which he mastered complete verbal proficiency in his languages by the time he was six. Alex learned some pre-reading English skills at home before learning to write in his French school. He had limited literacy skills by the time he was six years old, partial fluency in his languages by seven years old, and should become proficient in French and English literacy skills around nine or ten years old.

Learning occurs at a different pace in the Second Window, however (see Figure 6.8). Molly arrived in Switzerland from Canada at the age

Figure 6.8
The Second Window of Opportunity

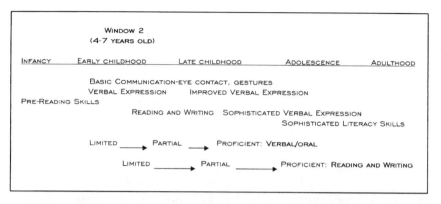

of four. She began attending an international school which was primarily in English but had several hours of French throughout the week which occurred in play-centered activities (role play, music, games). In her case, she was nearly proficient in English at four years old, but her French verbal skills were merely "limited." By late childhood (six or seven years old) she should have partial fluency in French, and by adolescence be a proficient bilingual. Molly's literacy skills differ in their stages from Alex's as well. Since Molly learned the English alphabet in her Canadian school, at four years old she already recognized most letters and most of their related sounds. She should learn to read competently in English in her international school at six years old, but will not be taught how to write in French until after third grade. By fourth grade she should have competent multiliteracy skills.

In the Third Window there is yet another change in the sequencing of skills (see figure 6.9). Whereas the acquisition of language abilities (understanding, speaking, reading, and writing) are spread out over childhood in the First Window, they occur simultaneously in the Third Window. For example, Laura arrived in the United States from Nicaragua when she was eight years old. When she began attending the public schools in the second grade she had to learn to speak, read, and write in English simultaneously. That is, English was learned as a "package deal." Shortly after uttering her first words (basic communication) she began to learn to read and write (literacy skills). Additionally, she was forced to learn to write in Spanish at the same time that she learned to do so in English as she had no exposure

Figure 6.9
The Third Window of Opportunity

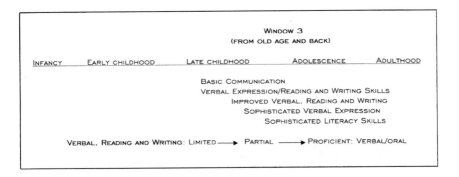

to writing before starting school in the United States. Once in Miami, however, she learned to read and write in Spanish in the school along with English. While Laura's story had a successful ending (she ended up getting her Master's in Business Administration from Stanford and now works for a prestigious bank), her disadvantage in comparison to Alex and Molly's cases should be clear. While the other children had the chance of learning verbal expression in their second languages in a relaxed, play-centered atmosphere, Laura had to learn both her native and second languages in the verbal and literate forms simultaneously. Laura faced a great deal of stress and pressure in the Third Window, though she fared well. Do all children do so well? No, many do not react favorably to such pressure and they do not succeed in becoming proficient bilinguals. Laura was highly motivated and had exceptionally supportive home and school environments in which to learn her second language, ingredients which were key to her success. These three cases show the clear benefits of acquiring a second language from birth (First Window), and if this is not possible, then in early childhood (Second Window).

As is apparent from the boxes above, all three of the Windows of Opportunity provide for the possibility of proficient language acquisition. However, by starting early in the First Window of Opportunity, children have several years where they build up of a variety of skills to become proficient. When learning a second language in the Second Window of Opportunity, children are conscious that they are undertaking a new language. Depending on their school system and previous home study, they may or may not be faced with learning to read and write in two languages simultaneously. This in and of itself is enough to discourage some children, though most do make it and become successful bilinguals. As an older person, learning languages in the Third Window of Opportunity forces us to learn to speak, read, and write concurrently. We adults approach the language on all fronts at the same time, but we already have solid skills in at least one language before we approach a new one. Children do not have the support of a fully established language to lean on when they do their learning, as they are still in the process of shoring up their mother tongue. In the First and Second Windows children have the chance of regarding a new language piece by piece. If not, they learn languages as adults do in the Third Window.

_____ *Chapter 7* _____

The Chefs and Chefs' Assistants: The Role of the Teachers and the Schools

ONE RARELY COOKS ALONE

We are often in the kitchen by ourselves, but rarely cook alone. Someone's influence is always on us. The same goes for our children and their languages. While you and the other family members may be the chefs in charge of your own family recipe for foreign language learning, you are accompanied, influenced, and helped by your children's teachers and the school(s) they attend. In some family cases, the entire job of teaching foreign languages is left to the schools, in other situations it is a partnership; whatever the case, you affect your child's schooling, and this schooling is affected by your child's home. In this chapter we turn to this very important aspect of foreign language learning and the mutually influential roles of teachers, children, and the schools they attend.

OPPORTUNITY AND SUPPORT IN THE SCHOOLS

Infant bilinguals, or those children who acquire two or more languages simultaneously from birth (the First Window of Opportunity), and child bilinguals who successively learn two languages (the Second or Third Windows) illustrate an important distinction in our discussion of Home and School Opportunity. The infant bilingual relies mainly on the Home and parents, while the child bilingual relies on the School for nurture, as well as a supportive home environment. Infant bilingualism is always successful—so far as I know, there are no unsuccessful attempts at rearing children bilingually from birth if the parents are consistent in their strategy of one-parent, one-language. Child bilingualism poses other challenges which are usually psychological in nature. However, "experience has shown time and time again that children in this situation will learn a second language with amazing rapidity if they are exposed to it" (Harding and Riley 1996:41).

We spoke at length about the role of Opportunity in the Home within the "Motivation" ingredient. Here we will describe what opportunities can take place for language learning within the schools.

The importance of your children's "second home," or school, is also a key factor in their success with learning another language. The support you receive from your school and especially your children's teacher(s) can in many cases make the difference in their motivation level and finally the outcome of their attempt at multilingualism. Schools can be extremely varied, and here we will limit our discussion to a very general description of three types: the international school, the "local" school, and the specialized language school.

International Schools

International schools generally claim respect for the variety of cultures their students come from as well as the languages spoken at home by their students. If the school itself is also a multiliterate environment, it is easily visible. Signs will be posted in all relevant languages showing that each one is considered important. A healthy respect for all the community languages should be a goal. The school will incorporate second language learning across all areas of the curriculum, not just during language hours. Reading daily to children in the school's languages should be the norm. Daily writing should be encouraged in the same languages the children are reading. Reading and writing themes should be related to other learning experiences across the school curriculum and directed to an audience beyond the teacher if possible. In the best case scenario all of these things occur, in the worst case scenario, international schools can become an exclusive ghetto, like a wealthy Los Angeles suburb in the middle of Country X. The aforementioned strong points of successful international schools should be a part of a family's evaluation process if international schools are an option.

Local Schools

The local school can come in a variety of shapes and sizes depending on the country, city, and community. The school language goals are quite different from international schools. The local school is usually interested in its students' achieving academic success, not necessarily cultural tolerance. And while such academic goals may include a "foreign language" requirement, subjects are usually taught in the community's dominant language. The "school culture" or "school philosophy" also has a great impact on whether or not a child is taught in a language-pure environment (no mixing of tongues by teachers), whether culture and other related aspects are taught in unison with language skills (Osborn 2000), and if children's natural curiosity about language is maximized for greater learning ease (Krashen 1996). Depending on the country, local schools may or may not provide new students with integrative support into the new environment and/or special classes to help them stay on top of academic issues while they master the language. Outside the U.S., in many cases, the local school is the seat of the typical "sink or swim" scenario with regard to the new language. Parents must monitor the progress of their child's language learning in such cases as her success with the new language will influence all other aspects of her school life. Whether your child is an immigrant in the U.S. bilingual or ESL program, or an "international student" in a multilingual school, the structure of the curriculum and the attitude the schools have about preserving cultural identity greatly influence a child's self-perception. Some parents resort to "extra classes" for their children with regard to the new language, leading us to the third type of school.

Specialized Language Schools

I was surprised to find that in my German night-school class there were three high school students. All had at least one year of German (one of them had six!) in the Swiss public schools but needed extra practice. Specialized language schools complement the structures of international and local schools, but by their very nature serve a different niche. For small children they may not even be an option. For adolescents, these language schools are an extra, paid out of the parents' pockets, and as such have a different type of motivation tied to them. I mention them here briefly as they are indeed another type of formalized language learning that can be used by families.

When Should My Child Learn to Read in a Second Language? What Research from Around the Globe Tells Us

In the United States and the United Kingdom it is not uncommon for pre-school age children (three-year-olds) to learn letters. By kindergarten (five years old) many of them are already reading. I remember, at three-and-a-half, my daughter was one of the last kids in her Cambridge, Massachusetts, pre-school to learn to write her name! By first grade reading is firmly in place, and writing is not far behind. In Latin America much depends on the type of school (public, private, religious), but generally speaking, reading is begun in kindergarten (five- and six-year-olds). In many European countries (Switzerland, France, and Germany, for example), reading and writing are taught starting at age six or seven in the first grade, and the Scandinavian countries at seven or eight years old. In Japan, children begin the long process of accumulating the minimal 1,980 characters needed to be considered "literate" very early on (three or so), but much of the teaching is left to parents (mothers in the home) until five or six years old. In any case, Theodore Andersson (1981) advises teaching literacy skills at home in the first language before the child enters school. Though this means that the parents have to take on the task of teaching letter sounds and names to their children, the rewards are worth it. Children come to the classroom already equipped with language tools which they are able to apply to the second language. They are more confident, and with good reason. Choosing whether or not to embark on the trail to biliteracy skills is really in the hands of each parent.

As most known cases revolve around children who learn to read and write in only one language system, it is hard to give "proven" advice about whether or not learning to read and write should be done simultaneously in two languages, or first in one, and then another with respect to literacy skills. I maintain that the age a child begins learning literacy skills is not as important as how separated it is from the subsequent literacy undertaking. In other words, it is not important if the native–English-speaking child learns to read and write in English at three, four, five, six, or seven years old, so long as she *later* learns to do so in French, not simultaneously. Studies of bilingual or multilingual societies shed some light on just when and how to teach literacy skills.

In *European Models of Bilingual Education* (Beardsmore 1993) various approaches to reaching the goal of biliteracy are described. I will share four such cases from this book to illustrate that while methods may vary, the key of separating multiple languages in time remains constant.

For example, in the German-minority schools in Denmark, Michael Bryman (Beardsmore 1993: 59) writes that for the first two years of schooling, Danish is introduced as an informal play lesson which gives Danish a status in the school. There is no attempt to teach the written language until the third year, when the acquisition of reading and writing has, in principle, been largely completed in German. This means that the children respect the Danish language, use it in play, but do not have formal training in it until three years after German literacy skills have been achieved.

In another example, the city of Brussels' Foyer project (Beardsmore 1993: 86–97) is used as a model. In the multicultural programs in the Dutch-language school system in Brussels there exists a fascinating combination of circumstances. In the early 1990s, Dutch-language kindergartens were composed of thirty-five percent Dutch-language families, thirty percent from mixed-language families (presumably Dutch and French), twenty percent from homogeneous French families, and fifteen percent from foreign families. This posed a very special situation in the Dutch schools, where just over a third of their children had Dutch as a first language. The fifteen percent foreign families include numbers of Italians, Turks, Moroccans, Spanish, and Armenians. The goal of the school system is that by the third year of schooling, ninety percent of the children are together in all subjects, with a small minority needing special classes. By the third year, literacy skills in the mother-tongue have been taught and Dutch lessons dominate. The goal is that the non-Dutch children learn to read in Dutch as a second language by their first year of elementary school (after three years of kindergarten "play" in verbal Dutch and their own native language). By the third to sixth grades children are expected to read and write in their native language, Dutch, and begin to do so in French.

Another example is from the small country of Luxembourg which requires that all its citizens go through a trilingual education system (Luxembourgish, German, and French). Although at birth the Luxembourger is monolingual, he soon becomes trilingual through schooling. The citizens of Luxembourg begin school at age five in the language of Luxembourgish, which is "progressively replaced by German" (Beardsmore 1993: 101–120). German is taught as a subject in the first grade and French is introduced in the second grade. In the United States' equivalent of the sixth through ninth grades, German is the medium, with French being taught as a subject, and mathematics is also taught in French. By the end of the ninth grade students are tri-literate in these languages.

In one last European example, author Hugo Baetens Beardsmore introduces the globalizing concept of the European School Model (1993: 121–154) which consists of nine schools attended by some 12,000 children. The largest school is in the Belgian capital and has 3,000 students. The school has "sub-sections" in eight official languages of the European Community Economic Commission. The school's philosophy is to not only reach literacy skills in a child's mother tongue, but compulsory second and third languages are required, with a fourth language being optional. Primary school instruction is in the child's first language, but a second language (usually English, French, or German) is also taught as a subject. Particular attention is paid to the first language and it is monitored in all lessons once the children have learned to read and write. The great importance of clarity of thought and expression in the native language is emphasized in this multilingual environment. Teachers of different languages are separated by time, place, and person. The child's second language is used to teach other subjects (physical education, music, art) in the third, fourth, and fifth grades of primary school—this is known as the Common Core Approach which we will go into in further detail in a moment. Writing in the second language is left until the sixth to eighth grades.

A final country example comes from perhaps the most studied bilingual school system in the world, Canada's, a system composed of two approaches: Early Total Immersion and Late Total Immersion. Early Total Immersion takes place from about five years old to second grade, and Late Total Immersion begins usually in seventh grade. In the English-dominant parts of Canada, Early Total Immersion children actually learn to read and write in French (their second language) before their first (English), which happens in the third grade.

In Late Total Immersion children learn to read and write in English first (in the first grade), and then in French (in the seventh grade).

While there are a good number of differences in these varying approaches to bilingual education, one shining consistency emerges. In each of these five cases of the German school in Denmark, the Foyer project in Brussels, the Luxembourg case, the European Schools, and the Canadian model, *writing skills in a second (or third) language were separated by at least a year from literacy skills in the first language*. This gives us as individual parents an indication about how and when to teach our own children to write in more than one language.

A very notable exception to this school approach to bilingualism is the fully bilingual school where children are taught to read and write in both languages in the same grade level. The key to success in these cases, however, is the separation in time (class hour), space (physical classroom), and person (different teachers for different languages). Additionally, many an adult polyglot who recalls learning to read and write in two languages simultaneously as being positive adds a word of praise about the teachers they had. Great teachers are part of every student's success story; it's unfortunate that this cannot be one factor that is always guaranteed! My husband offers one such example of learning multiliteracy skills in the same school year in a fully bilingual school. He first learned to read in Spanish and German (first grade), but with exceptional teachers who taught at different times of the day in different rooms. Six years later (seventh grade) he was taught English in school. Before attending a United States university he attended a semester-long program to refine his English literacy skills at the university level. Three years into his university studies he learned to read and write in French, and five years after that he learned to read and write in Japanese. By separating attempts at literacy by time, person, and place, he successfully acquired literacy skills in five different languages. Though both school systems can work (teaching multiliteracy skills simultaneously but separated by time, person, and place; or teaching multiliteracy skills separated by a full academic year or more), most international schools around the world choose the latter and separate the process by at least one year, and often more.

Learning to read and write in a second language is what we ask of many of our high school students in the U.S. public schools. In this case the multiliteracy task is obviously separated by several years (children learn to read and write in English first and then, often ten years later, learn to do so in a foreign language). My two sisters are cases in point. One learned to read and write first in her native English (at about five years old), then did so in French in high school at age sixteen. She graduated from the university with a degree in French History after successfully presenting her thesis in French and is currently a French and history teacher. The other sister learned literacy skills in her native English (at about age five), then in Spanish in high school (beginning at fourteen) and at the university level during college. She now regularly uses written Spanish in her law practice.

Whereas private language schools may or may not be an option, and where public school policies and structure may be rather set, your child's teachers may bring some flexibility into the picture, and this is where we turn to next.

OPPORTUNITY AND SUPPORT FROM TEACHERS

In all three school scenarios, teachers' preparedness in dealing with speakers of different languages is vital to the students' success. The Triad of Family, School, and Community mentioned in chapter 5 needs to be reiterated here. Outside of the First Window, when a child learns a foreign language it is a group effort. Obviously it is the child who will "own" the language, but he will achieve this best with a coordinated game plan where the Family, School, and Community have harmonious goals and strategies. Such a game plan is alluded to throughout this book, but a fuller description needs to be left for another book. Suffice it to say here that where the Triad is in unison about language goals, the children's work is simplified.

Most parents feel strongly about the role of their child's teacher. If the child feels secure and accepted in the classroom, then he can be free to focus on higher level tasks, such as learning a second language, write authoritative authors in the field (Allemann-Ghionda, Goumoëns, and Perregaux 1999). The following is summarized from a combination of sources related to bilingual education in the California schools and is a clear and simple summary of multilingual children's needs.

Teachers of bilingual children must provide their students with a program that gives them opportunities to feel secure, to feel accepted, to receive peer recognition, and to achieve success in learning. The teacher can assist in developing children's ego strengths through encouragement and sincere praise. It is especially important that the teacher maintain a happy, relaxed school atmosphere, one in which children are free to converse, to enjoy and share experiences, to use the language, and to feel free to speak even if they make mistakes, so long as they later correct them. A child is quick to sense a teacher's rejection of his language. Such rejection by the teacher can only serve as a barrier to communication between teacher and pupil. Along with the acceptance of the child's language, however, it is important for the teacher to help the child see that he must learn to use the new language in certain situations. The teacher who approaches the use of the languages or dialects in this way will find children with attitudes more conducive to learning to use their new language.

In other words, in the best of all worlds the teacher should have a healthy respect for the child's background and some idea of his language. At a minimum, the teacher should provide the child with a secure learning environment in which to tackle the language on his own.

What Teachers Can Do to Help Multilingual Children

Whether we are discussing people who are explicitly second language instructors or regular classroom teachers, there are some basic points that can be incorporated into the methods of instruction and they include the following, taken from research on bilingual classrooms. While no parent can impose his or her wishes on their child's teacher, there are some things that they can look for in the classroom setting. If the teacher seems receptive and appears open to ideas, then this list of general concepts devised by Dörnyei in his *Ten Commandments for Motivating Language Learners* (1996) may come in handy.

1. Make the language classes interesting by selecting varied and engaging topics, materials, and activities.
2. Have humor, fun, and games in the class.
3. Create a pleasant and friendly atmosphere.
4. Promote learner autonomy by allowing freedom in the classroom and sharing as much responsibility with the learners as you can.
5. Make the course relevant by doing a needs analysis and adjusting the syllabus accordingly.
6. Set a personal example of being motivated and committed yourself.

7. Develop the learners' confidence by encouraging them, giving them positive feedback, and making sure that they regularly have a feeling of success.

8. Make the foreign language "real" by introducing its culture, using authentic materials, inviting native speakers, and arranging native-speaking penfriends for your students.

9. Develop a good and trustful relationship with the learners.

10. Emphasize the usefulness of the knowledge of the foreign language.

While Dörnyei's work was focused on teachers in bilingual schools, his comments cross international borders and can be applied to instructors the world over at all age levels. Honing in on young children in the multilingual environment, there are vital differences between a foreign language classroom setting and the real communication needs of children. If the class can reflect the true communication needs of the children, they will learn the language successfully. This could mean letting the children discuss who is the greatest soccer player on earth (or the best rock star or what the latest clothing fad is), as opposed to doing the chapter on adjectives in the foreign language book—"he is the *best* soccer player because he is the *fastest*." In short, the class should reflect the real life needs of the children.

Some very specific activities could include the following, whether that be for an American child in an international school in Taiwan, or a newly arrived Turkish immigrant to Germany (paraphrased from various authors including works by Ching 1976; Goodman, Goodman, and Flores 1984; and Omark and Erickson 1983):

1. Develop a bond of trust and friendship between teacher and pupil. The child who trusts and likes his teacher will learn to respect his teacher and will want to win his approval. To develop this bond of trust and friendship, the teacher must show the child through actions and words that he likes him, respects him and his cultural background, accepts his language, believes in him, and expects him to succeed in learning activities selected to meet his needs within the school situation.

2. Provide an atmosphere which will encourage the child to share his culture and provide daily experiences and to talk about himself, his personal interests, and his aspirations. Until the child gains confidence and ease in speaking in the classroom situation, do not make comments such as "speak loudly so everyone can hear you" or "pronounce your words more clearly" or "look at your audience when you are speaking."

3. Provide books in the classroom library and display pictures and various artifacts relating to the cultural heritage of the child in order to reinforce self-identification.

4. Use a camera to take photos of class activities and to photograph individual pupils. Then use the photos to motivate oral, writing, and reading activities. This will also be helpful in the development of positive self-concept.

5. Develop a unit of study relating to the cultural heritage of the bilingual children. Have them bring to class and share materials they may have, such as stamp or coin collections, etc.

6. Give bilingual children many opportunities to be recognized by their peers, not only through sharing but also through academic accomplishments. Help children develop leadership abilities by providing them with situations in which they are chairpersons of committees or responsible for small groups, or within other areas that do not depend wholly on language, such as captains of sports teams.

7. Involve parents and siblings in class activities whenever possible to show the child that language learning is a family affair, and use the families as resources of information for the other language speakers in your class.

Research on Biliteracy

An interesting note about the mental process behind reading is found in Cole and Scribner (1978) who state that learning to read (the development of literacy) and reading itself (literacy) occur in the same way across cultures. Experts say that learning to read for the multilingual child and for the monolingual alike is effected by pre-reading skills, intelligence, maturation, visual and auditory activity, emotional stability, experiential background, educational opportunity, school attendance, readiness, and motivation to learn (Adams 1996). Such statements lead us to the conclusion that no special handling of the multilingual child needs to occur outwardly, as the process is the same all around the world, monolingual or multilingual. However, sensitivity to a child's background and what knowledge he brings with him to the classroom are vital for the teacher to keep in mind.

Teaching Strategies in a Multilingual Environment

After surveying hundreds of major bilingual programs in the United States, Doris Ching (1976) found that there were four main methods employed, two of which apply to multilingual schools around the world: 1) the Native Literacy Approach, and 2) the Common Core Approach. I will summarize them here briefly so that parents can recognize how their child's second language classroom is organized.

The *Native Literacy Approach* is based on the idea that the most efficient way of teaching children the community's dominant language is to first teach children to read in their native language, then (or simultaneously with the teaching of reading in the first language) teach the second language orally, and finally teach reading in the second language. The appeal of this approach is that by first teaching a child in his native language, reading instruction can begin at an earlier age than if the second language had to be taught first. The child's cultural heritage via his native language is preserved and learning to read is undertaken in the language with which the child is most comfortable. This is the example we saw earlier in the Brussels School Model.

The *Common Core Approach* teaches the new language through classes which depend more on physical demonstration or on numbers rather than on actual words. In such classes as science, computers, math, or physical education, children who are learning the community's language for the first time can do so in the "language of numbers," or through "kinesthetic" means which require a demonstration of physical qualities. After they are comfortable in these classes, which are somewhat less dependent on language for instruction, they can be integrated into other courses. This is used in the European Schools Model where the second language is used to teach physical education, art, and music in secondary school.

Native Literacy Approach	Common Core Approach
1) Read in native language first;	1) Learn oral skills in new language through classes less dependent on "words";
2) Teach new language orally;	2) Learn reading skills in the new language through direct exposure.
3) Teach reading in the new language.	

Though the approaches differ in their preservation of the "old" language, it is interesting that Ching found that "research studies show that there is no conclusive evidence that one approach is superior to another" in terms of learning to actually read in the new language. The main difference between the two has to do with whether or not the native language is *preserved* or *displaced*. This takes us out of the linguistic and pedagogical fields and more into the cultural, anthropological, and philosophical realms. Do the schools have a responsibility to preserve the cultural identities of the children they serve, or are they charged only with "educating" them?

The usefulness of Ching's findings in the context of this book is that parents can recognize what type of program is being utilized in their children's schools. If the Common Core Approach is used, then the orally bilingual child will learn to read and write only in the school's language. Parents will need to take on the task of reading and writing in the native tongue if literacy skills in more than one language is the goal.

What is essentially needed then is a teacher who understands, appreciates, and respects the cultural background of the child; who knows the phonics and grammatical differences between the child's native language and that of the second language being taught so that he can help the child with her linguistic needs; and who is knowledgeable of the various reading approaches available so that he will be able to select and utilize those that best meet the particular needs of the bilingual child. Who needs to do what? All three parties have a role to play:

Teacher	Child	Parent
1) Sensitivity to child's language background.	1) Know letters.	1) Supports child with resources and opportunity (basically providing books and the time necessary to practice reading skills).
2) Teach child the grapheme–phoneme relation of symbols to sounds.	2) Know phonetic alphabet.	
	3) Pre-Reading activities at home (developing a fondness for books and curiosity for letters).	

The studies we have seen here guide us with some very specific parameters. Children should learn some literacy skills in their native language before beginning school in order to facilitate their later "formal" learning in school. Practice at home can range from reading books to learning to recognize letter names and their sounds. Depending on the languages being learned, once the child masters the alphabet (or symbol system) of the language, she can then "expand" on her knowledge from home, rather than having to "learn from scratch" once in school. Once in school, literacy skills in different languages should be separated by time, place, and person. For those parents who are not yet convinced that multiliteracy is the way to go, the following section reviews the key areas of concern.

One Way to Influence a Bad Situation in School

In an instructive situation, my daughter's English teacher at her pre-school in Quito was "consistently inconsistent" in speaking to Natalie and her classmates. While most of the school day was spent in Spanish, the students received twenty minutes of English each morning where they sang and talked about the day of the week and the weather. The teacher was enthusiastic, but a non-native-English-language speaker. She taught the mainly Spanish-speaking group some vocabulary and simple songs in English. I believe Natalie was one of the only native-English speakers in the school, and so no one else seemed to mind the inconsistencies. While this type of exposure for monolingual children is most beneficial for learning the language later in life, the teacher's inexpertness could have been problematic for a bilingual like Natalie. Natalie was often confronted with differences between what was taught at home and what was taught at school. The words to nursery rhymes were a case in point: "row, row, row your boat, gently down the stream, merry merry merry merry *just a life a dream*" (instead of "merrily merrily merrily merrily, life is but a dream") was a simple mistake with words. But issues with basic syntax were a more pressing concern. Additionally, the teacher spoke to the children in English only during English time, so when they were on the playground or when she helped the other teacher during art hour, she did so in Spanish, creating a confusion in Natalie and in the other children as well, I presume. I spoke to the teacher about this and explained that Natalie was now committing grammatical mistakes that before were no trouble for her; confusing word order, for example. "I'm a little concerned about Natalie's English these days. She's coming home saying things like, 'what the weather is today?' instead of *'what is the weather like today?'*" The teacher was responsive and tried hard to correct these errors. She was bright and never made the same mistake twice, though new kinds of mistakes cropped up throughout the year. Each mistake in its own turn was quickly corrected. We made it through the year as good friends in the end, though I hope I never have to repeat such a relationship of parent-tutor again. I was extremely lucky that this teacher was so open. I have known (both as a parent and as a teacher myself) many an instructor who rejects any parental suggestions for change. In these cases each family has to gauge whether classroom harmony is valued more than the correction of individual grammatical quirks, though one would hope that teachers and parents alike are working towards the same goals.

With this final word about Teachers and Schools, we are now ready to focus on your individual family. What is your personal way of measuring the ingredients indicated in the previous chapters? How do the ingredients of the Windows and Aptitude fare in your house? Have you followed the basic baking instructions related to Motivation, Strategy, and Consistency? How strong are the Environmental Influences on your child's foreign language learning? Have you evaluated your daughter or son's multilingual brain carefully? And how do your child's teachers and school measure up against the "ideals" presented in this chapter? We turn to your family next.

Chapter 8

Baking Your Own: Your Personal Family Language Profile

DOWN TO WORK

Now it's time for you, the parent, to take stock of your own mixture. What is the combination of ingredients in your own child? What kind of tools do you have to work with in the kitchen? What is your own "recipe for success"? The following worksheet may help in terms of evaluating your personal situation (see Figure 8.1). It has also been used by teachers and other professionals to evaluate language difficulties that a child may be experiencing and to investigate the root causes. Try to answer each question with as much accuracy as possible and to reflect briefly on the ingredients and your own unique mixture as a family as you do so.

WHAT KIND OF MULTILINGUALISM DO YOU WANT FOR YOUR CHILD? THE DEGREES OF SUCCESS

Now that you have taken stock of your own family situation it should be apparent if an ingredient has been missing or if you have not made the most of some other part of the recipe. For example, if you realize that you are speaking a language to your child that is not your mother tongue, perhaps this could be the root of problems your child has been facing. Or if it is now clear that your child does not

Figure 8.1
Family Language Profile

◇ The mother's native/best language is _____. She speaks to her child in _____ (and _____).

◇ The father's native/best language is _____. He speaks to his child in _____ (and _____).

◇ (Answer only if applicable) Their regular nanny/caregiver/baby-sitter's best language is _____. (S)he speaks to the child in _____.

◇ The dominant language of the child's school is _____.

◇ The child receives instruction in (language) _____ in addition to the school's dominant language.

◇ The dominant language of the community is _____.

◇ The family language strategy in use is _____.

◇ The child is _____ years and _____ months old. Right now s/he is in the _____ Window of Opportunity.

◇ The child is a _____ boy _____ girl.

◇ The child has _____ brothers _____ sisters.

◇ The child is
_____ right-handed
_____ left-handed
_____ ambidextrous
_____ unclear which hand s/he prefers as of yet.

◇ The child learned his/her first language from birth.
The child learned/is learning his/her second language from _____ months/years old.
(Answer only if applicable:)

◇ The child learned/is learning his/her third language since s/he was _____ months/years old.

134

◇ The child learned/is learning his/her fourth language since s/he was _____ months/years old.

◇ The child has a _____ aptitude for language.
    High   Average   Low

◇ Personality-wise, the child is
    extremely shy   shy   average   outgoing   extremely outgoing

◇ The child is
    extremely motivated   somewhat motivated   not motivated   to learn his/her second/third/fourth language.

◇ The child has the opportunity to speak his/her first (best) language (check all appropriate choices)
    _____ at school   _____ at home   _____ with friends
    _____ with parents   _____ with relatives   _____ other

◇ The child has the opportunity to speak his/her second language
    _____ at school   _____ at home   _____ with friends
    _____ with parents   _____ with relatives   _____ other

◇ The child has the opportunity to speak his/her third language
    _____ at school   _____ at home   _____ with friends
    _____ with parents   _____ with relatives   _____ other

◇ The child has _____ books _____ videos _____ audio cassettes in his/her
    _____ first language   _____ second language
    _____ third language   _____ fourth language

◇ The languages the child is learning _____ share the same alphabet (A, B, C, etc.)
    _____ have the same linguistic roots.
    (check only if appropriate)

have many support materials (playmates, relatives, books, videos) in his second language, you could consider shoring up those areas where possible.

Next, families need to decide on the type, degree, or level of multilingualism they want for their child. To do this, let us return briefly to "Why" for a moment. Why do you want your child to be multilingual? The obvious responses are not enough once we reach this stage and think of long-term goals. What are some possible answers?

You want a multilingual child because "It will be good for his mind," and/or "So he can speak to his grandparents" and/or "It will help him play with the neighbor's kids," and/or "It will help him get into a good university in country X," and/or "It will help him get a job later in life." These are five very different but all very acceptable reasons for wanting to bring up children with more than one language. But reaching the goal of "being good for the mind" of a three-year-old is different from "speaking with grandma" at six, which is different from "helping them play with the neighbors" at ten years old, which is also different from getting into a good college at eighteen or finding a good job at twenty-four. Why are they so different? Because they return to our idea of different "degrees" of bilingualism in which there are different levels of achievement in the language. For some, speaking short, halting phrases is enough, for others, it is merely the beginning. In the latter case, having "some" competency is sufficient.

However, as Cummins (1978, 1980) writes, having some competency may not be enough. He states in his "threshold hypothesis" that knowing just enough to know you do not know that much can have negative effects. True, proficient bilingualism always has positive effects. "The threshold hypothesis assumes that those aspects of bilingualism which might positively influence cognitive growth are unlikely to come into effect until the child has attained a certain minimum or threshold level of proficiency in the second language. Similarly, if bilingual children attain only a very low level of proficiency in one or both their languages their interaction with the environments through these languages, both in terms of input and output is likely to be impoverished" (Cummins 1980: 6–7). Meaning the child who knows just enough to know he does not know that much can be faced with the dilemma of "semilingualism," or the lack of proficiency in his languages.

Let us continue reviewing our list of goals (see Figure 8.2). All of

Figure 8.2
Family Language Goals

1. We want our child to

____ speak well enough to be able to play with other children
       her/his age.   *Basic* Verbal
____ speak well enough to visit with our relatives in X country.   *Sophisticated*
____ speak well enough to be successful in school.   Verbal Skills

____ read in both his/her first and second languages.
____ read and write in both his/her first and second languages.   *Basic*
____ eventually read and write at university level in both languages.   Multiliteracy
____ eventually be able to work in either language   *Sophisticated*
       (understand, speak, read, and write with equal ability).   Multiliteracy
                                                       Skills

the cases call for good *oral skills*. The three-year-old and the six-year-old because they presumably do not have good writing skills at this point. Speaking is their main vehicle for communication; the ten-year-old as well because meeting his neighbors implies playing, *i.e.*, speaking, with them; the college student because of the nature of doing university work, which in the best case scenario, involves a verbal exchange of ideas; and the adult because speaking more than one language separates him from his competitors in the job market.

How do we define a "successful" bilingual? If our goal is verbal or oral proficiency in the language, then the young child who can speak two languages reasonably well has fulfilled the family goal of becoming a bilingual. The cases of the three-, six-, and even the ten-year-old are resolved by the ability to use another language in play. By having modest verbal exchanges (requesting or inquiring), the child has reached a level of bilingualism *for her needs*. For many families temporarily stationed abroad who know they will only be dependent on the new language for a limited number of years, this minimal level of proficiency (being able to speak with limited vocabulary in certain situations) is enough.

However, family goals change if the needs change. If a family has the goal of incorporating the use of the second language for life (as it is the father or mother's native tongue, for example) or if they hope to become fluent to the point of mastering *multiliteracy skills* (that is, managing to read and write in more than one language), a higher degree of proficiency is required. Once we decide the school-age child will learn to read and write in a second language, we are setting our

Figure 8.3
Active vs. Passive Bilingualism

Active Bilingualism	=	Speaking and Writing
Passive Bilingualism	=	Listening and Reading

goals for bilingualism higher than just desiring oral proficiency. The goal is moved further "upward" if we have hopes that our child will some day go on to university study in the new language (see Belcher and Briane 1995). This is also true if we believe he may find employment with his languages in the future.

"ACTIVE VERSUS PASSIVE" LANGUAGE LEARNING

A different way of categorizing the four skills of understanding, speaking, reading, and writing a language was pointed out to me by a good friend, Giselle Martínez de Meléndez. She calls this classification active bilingual goals (the ability to speak and write) versus passive bilingual goals (the ability to read and listen) (see Figure 8.3). While this is not the classical linguistic interpretation of "Active vs. Passive" bilingualism, it seems to illustrate a key point. The active bilingual goals require children to physically open their mouths and produce utterances (speak), and to take a pencil in hand and create meaningful scribbles (write). The passive bilingual goals allow the children to sit back and be read to or read themselves (listen), without having to "produce" anything. Each of these four processes is a separate (but related) complex learning step (see chapter 6 on the brain). Such a division makes for an interesting concept as it also relates to the order in which multilinguals lose their language skills if not practiced. I learned Japanese in high school and college and actively used it while studying at Sophia University over a summer, and then while we were stationed in Tokyo in my husband's diplomatic mission for three years. However, a few weeks ago (seven years since my last exposure to the language) I had the occasion to speak with a Japanese woman at a United Nations' function. While I understood her questions and comments (listening) without trouble, I found speaking a much greater task. Likewise, when she showed me a pamphlet written in Japanese, I was able to decipher (read) the main text about the

Galapagos Islands. If she had asked me to write the same thing I had just read I dare say I would have been hard-pressed to do so.

Being able to speak in two or more languages is by far the most common language goal and the most common achievement around the world. As we will see in the next section, learning to read and write in the second language is not nearly so common a feat. But for those families that do have reading and writing in more than one language as their goal, wise planning, coupled with good strategy, is necessary.

MULTILITERACY SKILLS

We now turn to the areas of Reading and Writing (Literacy) skills which compliment Speaking (Oral) skills in the scheme of foreign language learning. Whereas many researchers blend these three areas (oral skills, reading, and writing) together, recent studies indicate that each should be studied separately. We begin with the difference between the spoken and written word.

The Difference between the Spoken and Written Word

Unhappily, illiteracy is the norm worldwide, not the exception, so it should come as no surprise that there are more monolinguals who speak their single language than learn to read or write it. Similarly, most bilinguals in the world *speak* two languages but few read and write in more than one, if that. To take this point even further, "Most of us come from families that four generations ago did not possess the ability to read," claims Geschwind (1982: 22). "It is only in the past 100 years or so that universal literacy has been declared an aim of many societies," writes Ellis (1994: 75). Given the elusive goal that literacy is, why should we be concerned about *which* language our children become literate in? Shouldn't we just be pleased that they learn to read at all?

Learning to read and write are exceptional accomplishments. The differences between the spoken and written word give us some indication of why literacy is such a challenge. Simply speaking in one's native tongue is an amazing mental feat (one that distinguishes us from all other animals on earth, to be exact), the ability to read and then to write draw our awe even further. Speaking is transient, temporary, fleeting. The written word is intransigent, permanent, in short, a record. Snow and Ninio (1986) write that the spoken language implies a social interaction, while the written word is decontextualized. The differences in the spoken and written languages go even farther than the mouth or the pen. An additional mental step occurs in the brain between reading and writing (see chapter 6). I have constructed a diagram based on Calfee's (1977, 1984, 1986) distinctions between the spoken and written word which help us visualize these differences (see Figure 8.4).

Here we see that while the written word is rather "binding," there is a freedom and flexibility about the spoken word which allows us to jump from one topic to another. But the spoken word does not compare to the written word when it comes to aiding our memory. What is written "in black and white" can be repeated over and over, exactly the same way, whereas the spoken word can change with circumstances.

While both are a part of human language, it is clear that the spoken and written word are distinct in their functions in our lives. Perhaps this gives us the reason as to why oral proficiency is much more common than literacy skills in a foreign language. How are literacy skills taught, then, and in what ways does it differ from the spoken word which seems to come naturally to children? This is the focus of the next section.

The Great Debate about How to Teach Reading

An article in the *New York Times* Nation Section on Sunday May 11, 1997 was titled "Teaching Children to Read: Politics Colors Debate Over Methods." This article made it clear that there is yet to be a consensus on the best way to teach reading to any child, let alone a multilingual one. The 42nd Annual Convention of the International Reading Association was composed of 15,000 reading teachers and educators who gathered in Atlanta to answer the question, "What is the best way to teach children to read?" This conference reflected the division that has existed in the United States for the past fifty years. In a nutshell, the two camps are divided into those who are inclined towards the phonic or "sound it out" method, and those who are "Whole Language" advocates, who encourage students to find

Figure 8.4
The Spoken vs. Written Word

Natural Language (utterances)	Formal Language (text)
Highly implicit	Highly explicit
Context bound	Context free
Unique	Repeatable
Idiosyncratic	Memory Supported
Personal	Impersonal
Intuitive	Logical, Rational
Sequential Descriptive	Expository Content

more meaning in what they read even if it means guessing at how the word is pronounced.

In her recent book *Beginning to Read, Thinking and Learning about Print*, Marilyn Jager Adams (1996) in conjunction with the Reading Research and Education Center at the Center for the Study of Reading at the University of Illinois, Urbana-Champaign, was charged with a United States Congressional mandate to provide guidance on beginning reading programs. While her research was concerned with English-only readers, the information she provides is valuable in viewing the multilingual child as well.

Adams points out that historically, the earliest methods of reading instruction in Colonial times in the United States followed a straightforward, two-step process: Teach the code, then have them read. Phonics is the "system of teaching reading that builds on the alphabetic principle, a system of which a central component is the reaching of correspondences between letters or groups of letters and their pronunciations" (51). In contrast, children who learn through a "see and say" or "whole language" method were slower in decoding unknown words, though they surpassed phonics-taught children in initial reading speed. In studies the "phonics children, however, not only caught up with but surpassed their look-say peers in silent reading rate, comprehension, and vocabulary by the end of the second grade" (38). Based on this information, we will assume children will be learning to read through a phonics-based system when we compare English-only to multilingual children and reading skills. It is interesting to note that while the Americans have been hotly contesting the virtues of phonics, the British have never left the system and remain true phonics believers to the end, as do the French and the Germans.

What Is Important for Pre-Readers? Know Your Letters!

Adams' review of the literature related to pre-readers came to some clear conclusions: "knowledge of the letter names was found to be the single best predictor of first-year reading achievement, with the ability to discriminate phonemes auditorily [the sounds that go with the letters] ranking a close second . . . these two predictors were the winners regardless of the instructional approach administered" (Adams 1996: 55). Helping your child know the alphabet is a big step towards later reading skills. Once that is achieved, relating the phonetic sounds that go with each letter comes next.

The third best predictor was mental age as measured by the Pinter-Cunningham Intelligence Test (55–56). This is important for policy makers in the United States as well as for parents abroad who are unsure about when they should introduce reading to their children, especially if the school system they are in waits until six or seven years old to begin teaching literacy skills. It was not uncommon just a generation ago in the United States (and still true throughout Europe with the exception of the UK) that reading and writing skills were taught in the first grade, when the child was six or seven. (Interestingly enough, if you recall, this seven-year bench-mark is also where our Second Window of Opportunity closed.) Waiting until a child has reached the age of six-and-a-half or seven to begin writing was once thought to benefit the child as it kept the complexities of the written word at bay. However, researchers such as Coltheart (1979) "showed that the studies on which this claim was based simply could not bear the weight of the conclusions placed upon them" (quoted in Ellis 1994: 76) and showed in another series of studies that early letter recognition made up for low mental age (that is, a seven-year-old who did not measure seven mentally but who knew the alphabet was able to make up lost ground). Knowing letters allowed children to catch up regardless of their lower mental age indicator. This is a strong argument for starting sooner. As has been reiterated by researchers for both monolinguals and multilinguals alike, poor reading is related to poor academic progress over the whole of a child's academic life. Reading is the key to success, and an early start in knowing letter names and the sounds behind them is the key to reading.

The following are some suggestions for parents to enhance their child's language development which I devised for my bilingual English reading students.

Ten Practical Suggestions for Parents to Enhance Pre-Reading Skills in Children

1. *Read with your child*, preferably letting her choose the book. Read in an interactive way, ask questions about the text, ask your child to find the pictures related to the passage being read, suggest alternative possibilities to an ending, reflect on the content of the book, let her turn the pages—reading for 30 minutes a day has been shown to boost verbal expression and vocabulary skills in children as young as two! These are both directly related to later reading skills. Ask your child to "read" you the story even if it means retelling from memory. Point out key words if she asks. Read in as many languages as you are proficient in.

2. *Play* with *Nursery Rhymes* and use *Rhythmic Games* to encourage phonemic awareness (in as many languages possible). This could also include nursery rhyme tapes in other languages as the rhythm, intonation, and variety of sounds are intriguing to children, especially during the Windows of Opportunity.

3. *Sing* with your child. Or encourage him to sing alone. It is engaging and encourages memory, and shows benefits much the same as rhythm games and rhymes (in as many languages as your child shows interest).

4. *Ask* your child to *retell a story* from a book or to make up a story herself and then listen, ask questions, and show your interest in her blooming literary development!

5. Try *"Reading"* games in the car or while at the supermarket. ("Today is 'M' day. How many M's can we see on the labels of the food or on license plates or on street signs?" Make sure you repeat the sound of the letter of choice each time they find it. "Yes, another 'M' mmmmmmm, good!" Or a game of "I Spy" is always a winner: "I spy a red train, who sees the train?" If you see signs in other languages, be sure to read them as well, if you are capable. Be sure your pronunciation is good in all languages you play the game in.

6. If available, Sesame Street-type *videos or cassettes* which encourage letter and sound recognition can be used;

7. Playing with magnetic letters on the refrigerator or cutting shapes from playdough allow the *physical manipulation of letter shapes*.

8. *Pretending to write* (play restaurant with your child and let him "take your order" on a small note pad, for example, or play "school" or "library" with him to show the many different ways reading and writing are used around him. Teach your child to actually write and recognize his own name as well as that of other family members (mom, dad, etc.).

9. *Labeling* some (by means not all!) things in the child's room ("table," "chair," "door") helps with later sight recognition of words.

10. *Encourage all your child's attempts and do not compare her progress to others.* Each person has different strengths and aptitudes, and your positive reinforcement is necessary to help her reach her own potential.

Remember: Readers come from reading families. Studies have shown that children who see their parents reading are more likely to be readers themselves. Model the behavior you want to encourage.

Where does that lead us in teaching reading and writing skills to multilingual children? For one, it means starting early so that multiliteracy skills can be achieved. But how is this actually done? Depending on the second language being learned, different steps should be taken.

The Case of the Roman Alphabet

For those children coming from English-speaking backgrounds who are learning European languages (or those with a Latin or Germanic base) which use the Roman or Phoenician ("A, B, C . . .") alphabet, it would seem logical to suggest that a good rule of thumb is that they should learn the phonics or sounds in (one of) their native language(s) first, as is most natural for the child and parent. This can be done while reading at story-time, or when the child's curiosity is piqued and she asks what a certain letter is. After the child knows her native language alphabet (the A, B, Cs in English), and the phonic alphabet ("ahh," "buh," "kuh," "duh," etc.), she can expand the phonic alphabet to include the letter-sound relationships of the second language *as if they were part of the large group of exceptions*. For example, English-speaking children should learn that "E" in English is like the "e" in "egg," but that there are exceptions as with the word "me."

Similarly, "e" in French (or Spanish or German or Italian) is pronounced in "thus-and-such" a way. This means that the child builds
on an existing set of symbols (the A, B, Cs) as opposed to starting
from square one (or the letter "A"), all over again. Children's work
is economized as they learn the actual letters once, not twice. They
only add the different sounds (usually the vowels and a small number
of consonants).

The Case of the non-Roman Alphabet

In ideographs, or pictograph, cases, the brain receives the word in
a different area due to its visually distinct form which is more like a
drawing than a letter. The pictograph or *kanji* for "sun" 日 in Japanese
looks like the sun rising in a window (or so said my Japanese instructor!). In many ways this is much more logical in the mind of a child
when learning to write because he can draw a person or the sun or a
spider or a flower before he attempts letters which have no logical or
obvious connection with the sound they are associated with. This
makes the Japanese and Chinese pictographs of a completely different
nature compared with their alphabet counterparts, and happily one
that small children find "logical" in many cases. While the learning
of which strokes (lines) must be done in what order to write a character has its own confusion (for native Japanese speakers and foreigners alike), the chances of confusing the written symbol with a sound
in the native language is not generally a problem.

The Japanese *kana*, or syllabaries, are like the Roman alphabet.
Visually they have no correlation to the sounds they make and must
simply be memorized. This is similar to other writing systems such
as Hebrew, Arabic, Greek, Urdu, Sanskrit, and Korean systems that
will be completely unfamiliar to the Roman alphabet-using child.
Their saving grace is that they, too, have a finite number of symbols
to attach to sounds (usually between twenty-five and forty-five), so
the goal is to plow through them one by one. This can be quite
arduous for the parent who may also have to learn the writing system
along with the child in order to be helpful. Learning these alphabets
and their corresponding sounds is the first important step in helping
your child become literate in her new language.

Aside from these orthographic differences, which are big enough
in and of themselves, should teaching multilingual children differ

from teaching monolingual children in any other way? And how do we get from "Pre-Reading" to actually "Reading"?

Beyond Pre-Reading Skills

Once a child begins to read well on her own (which can vary greatly, but which on average is about eight years old), the only way for her to become more efficient is practice. Professor Alfonso Carramazza at Harvard University spoke of a stroke patient who could name all letters in a word but could not read the word nor pronounce it nor could he tell the meaning. At this stage of emergent literacy we recognize a word as a single unit, not by all of its letters, *and* we read whole concepts, not word for word. Ellis states that reading in its natural state is not done word by word, but rather by reading sentences that link up to form passages of coherent, connected text which informs, instructs, and entertains (Ellis 1994). Given the ability to read quickly and effortlessly as a general goal of reading, where does that leave multilingual children?

What Contributes to Reading Ease?

According to Carramazza and Ellis, the three key factors that contribute to reading speed, ease, and comprehension are *Familiarity*, *Repetition*, and *Frequency*. Good readers read a lot, in whatever language. Multilingual children face the challenge of reading lots in all the languages they hope to improve. While increases in oral vocabulary in one language tend to reflect increases in vocabulary in the second language, reading skills do not have such transferable benefits. When reading, each language must be practiced on its own time. This means that the multilingual child has the added need to practice her reading skills in all of her languages on a regular basis or they will not thrive. This goes one step further when we progress to writing.

Getting to Writing

Writing, unlike reading, which is a decoding and labeling process, is both a product and a process in itself. The same three areas of the brain execute reading and writing, but in the opposite order. Writing adds an additional step at the end which is the mechanics of writing itself (taking a pen to paper). Content and form both need attention.

Both the quality of what is written and how it is written are important. Learning the correct symbols in each language and the correct stroke order to create those symbols is the heart of the process. What is said, and how thoughts are formulated and passed on to paper, leads to the content. It has been said in the educational field that "writing is a form of thinking," and the exercise of composition itself helps create thought. Helping multilingual children learn to write means not only being sensitive to the mechanics of writing, but also to this mental process. While many researchers have addressed the topic of *multiliteracy* (Saville and Troike (1971), Rosier and Farella (1976), Titone (1977a), Andersson (1981), Kielhofer and Jonekeit (1983), Cumming (1994), and Belcher and Briane (1995), to name a few) it is hard to sift through the literature and find "the" method of achieving writing skills in more than one language, and so once again we pull together the pieces and see what kind of a puzzle we end up with.

IN WHICH LANGUAGE SHOULD MY CHILD LEARN TO READ?

For those parents raising multilingual children in foreign countries, the question of whether or not our children should learn to read and write in their native language or in that of the school system (or in both) is a pressing concern. The literature in this field is sparse at best and the conclusions here are based on a collection of cases as opposed to hard fact.

The most common scenario, note Harding and Riley (1996: 13), is that the "typical" bilingual only learns to read and write in the language of the school. For many this is enough. The schools take on the responsibility of teaching reading and writing and that is the end (in the simplest of cases) of the family concern about the matter. But this has its drawbacks as many a parent can sympathize. If the child learns to read and write exclusively in the language of the school, then she is "handicapped" on her return to her home country and native language. If the child has no plans of leaving the new language community this is not a problem, but many internationally mobile families do eventually "return home." So, what happens if the family decides that they want their child to learn to read and write in their native language, whether it be for the benefit of communicating with their relatives abroad, or for the simple pleasure of reading in the language of their choice? This leads us to the indicators of when schools around the world begin teaching children to read and write.

How can parents living abroad foster multiliteracy skills? A final example that had its genesis in a parent initiative might be helpful in giving us an answer.

A Group of Parents Working to Foster Biliterate Skills in Their Children

An excellent example of a creative community effort to teach multiliteracy skills separating the languages by time, space, and person is the Playgroup Reading Programme in Ferney-Voltaire, France. While this type of program is not a possible alternative for many families abroad, the philosophy behind the program's structure is worth discussing here.

Families who spoke English at home but whose children attended local schools in this area of France and nearby Geneva agreed that there was a "gap" in their children's learning. Most felt their children were behind peers of similar age in the United States and the United Kingdom in literacy skills, which are taught much later in France and Switzerland. In 1993 a reading program was designed and headed by Liz Caloghiris to meet the needs for more formal English instruction for these families. This evolved into an all-volunteer group of six qualified teachers to tutor children in English at four different levels. A key working variable in this community solution to the problem of balancing reading proficiency in the native language and that of the community (French) was, again, Timing. As French and Swiss schools teach reading at age six or seven, the Playgroup Programme starts at age four. This gives the children one to three years to gain reading and writing proficiency in English before learning to do so in French. If the French or Swiss schools started their writing programs any earlier, it is questionable whether the Playgroup Programme would enjoy as much success as it does. The Playgroup Reading Programme example highlights the importance of separating language instruction when it comes to multiliteracy skills.

A Good Writer in One Language Is Bound to Be a Good Writer in Another

Again, a child's personal aptitude, her motivation, and the opportunities she has all should come into consideration when learning multiliteracy skills. But how does it actually work in practice? In the cases cited earlier it is obvious that those people have a high aptitude for languages as they managed to learn multiliteracy skills. But why the division between those who can write easily and those who find it burdensome to learn?

The correlation between one's ability to write well in one's native language and one's level of verbal proficiency in the second language is an important factor here. That is, good native English writers who are also good Spanish speakers will presumably have a "good" chance at learning proficient writing skills in Spanish. Writing performance in a second language is influenced both by mother-tongue writing expertise and by proficiency in the second language (Cumming 1994: 173). This is presumably why the European School Model devotes a great deal of attention to ensuring that each child's first language skills are carefully monitored, and why we as parents need to do the same with our own child's mother tongue.

MAKING THE DECISION TO TEACH YOUR CHILD BILITERACY SKILLS

Many factors should be considered by parents when deciding in which language and when to teach reading skills to their multilingual children. First, parents must return to their family goals which were discussed in the previous section. Do you as a parent feel it is necessary for your child to learn to read and write in more than one language? Are you willing to monitor multiliteracy skills throughout your child's education? Is there really a choice in the country where you reside?

Depending on what the reading and writing practices are in the country where you find yourself, your child's spoken proficiency in the school language, your confidence in your personal abilities to aid your child's reading skills (or to find someone who can), and your child's age, a decision can be reached. You as a parent have to decide in which language to pursue literacy depending on which country you live in (whether or not your school is an early or late starter), the similarities of the languages, and whether or not it is important to you whether your child knows how to read and write in your native language.

In our family, for example, we decided that because of the relatively late start in teaching reading and writing in the German School (first grade), at age five our daughter began learning to read in English in a special program designed for and taught by native English language speakers. With one year of English reading and writing study, her transition into German reading and writing was eased considerably. Her solid foundation in English, which has a phonic alphabet not completely dissimilar to German, gave her an edge when she began learning to read in German. Having Spanish as a native language was also a help phonetically. For example, "O" in German is the same as the English "O" in "orange"; "I" in German was the same as the Spanish "I," and so on. Spanish reading and writing will be home taught after German is fully established. Such decisions must be made on a family by family basis. If the school will teach literacy skills in a language the family is content with then that may be the end of the discussion. However, if the family goal is for multiliteracy skills, it may become necessary to undertake some of the instruction at home.

Maintaining Literacy Skills in a Native Language

If a second language is learned after reading and writing is already established in the native language (in the Third Window), Harding and Riley (1996: 147–148) offer some practical suggestions in maintaining writing skills in the native language: "Games are the best incentive: one example is 'treasure hunts.' . . . The children can also write to the family [back home] . . . creating cartoon strips . . . mak[ing] 'real' books for a younger child . . . make children read aloud the letters received from the family and friends."

The tried-and-true method of using language as a game and for play is always a good idea. The importance of maintaining reading and writing skills in the native language(s) has to be decided by the parents, but it would seem unfortunate to "lose it" once a child has worked so long and hard to learn it in the first place. The following section offers an example of a multilingual child's mental processes as she begins to learn to read.

A STORY OF A MULTILINGUAL CHILD LEARNING TO READ

Natalie Is Learning Letters (August 29, 1998)
Geneva

Natalie will have an after school class once a week in reading skills in English at the Playgroup Reading Programme in France. Natalie is a child who will speak circles around most people, but she has a very special mind when it comes to reading. She has an amazing auditory memory for songs, composers' names, all the lines in a book (so she can feign reading when in fact she is retelling the story she heard). And she is gifted in recalling having visited a certain place, or where we parked the last time we were at the zoo, etc., people's faces, dance steps learned in ballet, or the pattern on the teacher's dress that morning. But curiously enough she can't remember right and left, or where the table is in a restaurant if she gets up to go to the bathroom (poor spatial location). Now, whether related or not neurologically, Natalie is also weak in remembering forms, or more specifically, letters and numbers. She was desperate to dial the new neighbors' phone number, but when I dictated "776–5928" to her she had to begin at the number one and count through all the numbers to get to the "7." The same goes with the alphabet. If she asks, "How do you spell 'Espinosa'?" and I say "E" she has to go through "A," "B," "C," "D" before she gets to "E" and can write it. (Needless to say this is exasperating when we get to the "S" and the "P"). This is a very interesting and frustrating phenomenon, I feel. Is it possible that she has learned the twenty-six letters of the alphabet as a single unit? As she has learned the numbers one through nine? When we try using phonics and matching sounds to letters and letter names there is even more confusion. There is a five step process to go through with her:

1. Say the sound;
2. Match the sound to a letter name;
3. Remember what the letter looks like;
4. Remember the lower-case vs. capital form of the letter;
5. Repeat the sound (by this time she has usually forgotten it!).

Though fascinating, this has made learning the alphabet a chore as opposed to the *"alegría"* felt when she learns a new song, a new dance, a new game, a new spoken language. Strangely enough, she is very good (for her age) at math. She will often stare out into space while we're driving somewhere, and comment off-handedly that "two plus two is four and five plus three is eight and four plus four is also eight." So her numerical concept and understanding are there, as is her syntax ability and fluent pronunciation in three different languages, but her ability to encode these into written form is a much larger task than learning to speak.

Could any of these problems arise because phonetic relations require the one-to-one matching of a sound to a letter and in her case she has too many sounds that match to too many letters ("ee" in English is "E" but in Spanish it is "I")? She will not learn how to read and write in German for another year, though letter recognition is taught next year. For now, she will only learn to read in English. To be honest I don't think she could handle learning to read in more than one language at the moment, though I believe that speaking on a daily basis in several languages can only be beneficial.

This diary entry touches on many of the key points discussed in this chapter on multiliteracy skills and highlights the child's perspective on the language learning. As this short description illustrates, it is not an easy process, but yes, a manageable one. When a family decides that reading and writing in more than one language is the goal, it is kind of like opting for the fancy soufflé instead of sticking to the box cake mix. It does require more effort, but it is well rewarded.

For your child, showing that you appreciate the effort and understand the difficulties she has in learning a new language are important. Your empathy for the process, and your understanding of the challenges mean a great deal to your child. But problems can and do arise.

We now turn to the area of language learning that parents in general would rather not have to face. What happens when difficulties come up? When are the languages themselves to blame? Is it ever the better choice to "drop" multilingualism in favor of a "simpler" lifestyle? We turn to these questions in the following section.

Chapter 9

A Mess in the Kitchen

THE HIDDEN DISASTER

While we are all trying to do our best by our children, and in our kitchen, sometimes the sloppy cook within us emerges. However, when your kitchen is a mess it's clear; when your child's language undertakings have become messy, it is less obvious.

WHAT TO DO IN PROBLEM SITUATIONS

What happens when a parent has "done everything right" and there is a problem? What if the child is delayed in speaking? What if he does not speak at all? What if he mixes languages beyond the normal time-frame? What happens if he only uses the grammar from one of the languages although he has perfect control over the vocabulary? What if the child refuses to speak in one of the languages at all? What if dyslexia crops its ugly head in the middle of our writing process? What if the school does not cooperate in your efforts and the teacher has no sensitivity towards your child's special case? What if the child has unclear speech or stutters? Should we take a closer look at the "old research" which discouraged multilingualism in the 1950s?

To begin to answer all of these questions we need to take a wider view of what multilingualism is, and what it implies when speaking about our children's overall intelligence.

Do Four Languages at Five Years Old Help or Hurt Cognitive Development and the Child's Intelligence?

Since we all agree that at least one of our goals is to lead our children to the riches of multilingualism without suffering the pitfalls, let's go back to the basic arguments for and against child multilingualism. We know there are benefits; are there any costs? Let us begin by addressing some general concerns about the "mental burden" of multilingualism.

I have often wondered why so many people shy away from the chance for their children to learn a second (third or fourth) language. Or if they "don't mind" their children being bilingual, why do they allow children to do so by chance and without actively participating in their child's development with the languages? A related question is that if we do decide to teach monolinguals another language, why do we begin doing so in our public schools so late? And if multilingualism is "good," why has it taken so long for the stigma around immigrant bilinguals in schools to change?

The Reasoning Behind the Two Opposing Camps

Parents against Multilingualism

In speaking to parents I have heard many concerns: "Learning another language will be too much for him"; "Too many languages will confuse her"; "He's just not ready"; "My daughter just isn't good at languages"; or "I don't want him to get behind in his first language because he's learning a second one." A common worry regarding second language acquisition is that teaching too many languages at one time will somehow "overload" the brain and lead to life-long learning problems. Is it possible that all these well meaning mothers and fathers could be right? Yes, it is. But interestingly enough, it could be that their opposing camp is *also* correct.

Parents in Favor of Their Children Learning a Second Language

The other camp is the group of people who push the idea that a second language opens up the brain to greater stimulus, that one's chances of thinking with a wider scope are heightened, that making friends from other lands and enjoying movies and books and customs from other countries is increased with the ability to speak another tongue. Not to mention the later marketability of polyglots in comparison with others in today's work force. The opinions on the subject run strong, and everyone has a story to share.

Some Stories from Both Sides of the Fence

While standing in front of her bakery and ice cream shop in a clean, flower-filled street in Quito, Ecuador, my friend Danielle tells me I should not be concerned about my son's lack of vocabulary at age two. She says (as she greets a customer in French, then another in German) that she was just the same, and it was because of the number of languages surrounding her in infancy. Her mother, who is German, and her father, who is French, migrated to Ecuador where they speak Spanish. She says that she didn't open her mouth to speak until she was three, at which time all three languages came spewing out in equal fluency.

Later that day I receive a concerned couple in my office who begin explaining their worries to me (in a mixture of Spanish and English) about their daughter. Maria's parents blame her current dyslexia and shyness on the fact that she had always heard Spanish, Hebrew, and English as a mix since she was little. And now, they fear, she is "handicapped for *vida*."

And then there is Rhama, who was mentioned earlier in the example of high aptitude learners. Her father is Indian and her mother is Japanese. She speaks Hindi, Japanese, and English with no accent and has never found there to be a confusion with her languages.

How could *all* these cases be true?

The "Old" Research

Many of the arguments against teaching children a second language were based on intelligence tests conducted in the 1950s on immigrant populations of all ages arriving from southern Europe to the United States who subsequently learned English. To determine the validity of these "intelligence tests" we should first understand this group's history. Why were these people immigrants in the first place? Probably not because they wanted to come to the United States to learn "English as a Second Language," but rather, they were in search of better economic opportunities, coming from poorer backgrounds, and English "just happened to them" as an aside to their primary goal of improving their livelihood. While similar economic immigrants exist today, our current discussion is on fostering the cognitive abilities of the young to create multilingual children with the emphasis on *adding* new knowledge (i.e., a language), not on *deleting* it (i.e., subtracting a language and replacing it with English) as happened in many immigrant cases.

Another argument against early second language learning revolves around the question of "brain overload." Wouldn't we be better off just using what "brain space" we have devoted to language to completely develop our mother tongue? Aren't there a number of bilinguals who are less than "fluent" in either of their languages? Linguist–sociologist Skutnabb-Kangas calls this *semilingualism* as opposed to monolingualism or bilingualism. These poor souls never fully develop proficiency in their first language, and therefore do not have a language in which to think profound thoughts or to express what they do think with clarity. What is the point of speaking many languages poorly, when we can focus on speaking just one brilliantly? Others refute this by citing how scientists now know that humans use approximately twenty percent (some more, some less) of the brain's potential. That is, synapses occur between just twenty percent of the neurons we are born with. Given how much potential is left for development, should "overloading" children still be a concern? No, *nein*, *non*, say many polyglots. French linguist Claude Hagège (1996), who speaks a couple dozen languages himself, writes that this should not be a concern. Bilingual people who express themselves poorly would probably have been monolinguals who expressed themselves just as poorly, some people just have poor verbal expression, he argues. Neurologists boost the idea that there is no known limit on the number of languages the human brain can take in. What is clear now, is that multilinguals use more of their right hemisphere than monolinguals, who generally have their language centered in the left hemisphere. This leads us to the idea that rather than "overloading" the brain, the multilingual is using parts that would otherwise go unemployed.

Along with the peaks and valleys, there are many plateaus along the path towards bilingualism. François Grosjean writes in *Life With Two Languages, An Introduction to Bilingualism* (1982) that there are many easily labeled stages of an "early" bilingual's language development to include: "the initially mixed language stage; the slow separation . . . and increasing awareness of bilingualism; the influence of one language on the other when the linguistic environment favors one language; the avoidance of difficult words and constructions in the weaker language; the rapid shift from one's dominant language to another when the environment changes; the final separation of the sound and grammatical systems but the enduring influence of the dominant language on the other in the domain of vocabulary" (181). Her brief summary of the many stages on the road to articulate fluency in a second language highlights the human "highs and lows" that are part of a natural process. Parents faced with a "low" are often tempted to abandon multilingualism, as they fear for the overall well-being of their child. What we have learned is that this is generally unwarranted.

As stated earlier, there are different ages when the brain is "better prepared" to receive a foreign language successfully. When those opportunities are missed, problems arise. So how do we know when we are faced with a "real problem" versus a "missed opportunity"?

First, parents should take a deep breath and stand back for a moment. Do not fall into the trap of blaming the gift of multilingualism for what may be normal developmental stages in your child. George Saunders (1988) relates many sad cases where advice by professionals went wrong. Such cases include a story about his own son to whom Saunders himself had spoken exclusively in German (a second language for him which he claims to speak fluently). The clinician who had examined the boy for fifteen minutes advised Mr. Saunders to speak to his bilingual three-year-old exclusively in English as so many languages were obviously a "mental burden" on the child. Saunders acknowledges that his child failed to answer many of the doctor's questions, but this was due to his son's shy character, not because of his lack of language, something the clinician did not take note of during the brief examination. Similarly, Traute Taeschner (1983) writes of a case where a pediatrician advised a German mother to stop speaking German to her Italian-German child (in Italy). The doctor believed that his language development at eighteen months was delayed. The mother followed the doctor's advice and lo and behold, at twenty months the child started speaking. This is a case of a false correlation. Whereas many children begin speaking their first words around their first birthdays, it is not abnormal for others to do so in the second, and some even in the third year of life. Sadly enough for this mother and her child, the "delayed" speaking which the doctor diagnosed forfeited the child's chance at another language and the closer communication ties with his mother. It is most probable that this individual child would have begun speaking at twenty months whether he had one, two, or ten languages surrounding him.

Bilingualism does not cause dyslexia or stuttering. Wendell Johnson's research on stuttering does not even entertain the idea. Harding and Riley (1996) also note that countries with high levels of bilingualism do not have high levels of stuttering. These and other myths work to prejudice parents and the community against the gift of bilingualism. One should not be too quick to label a child's difficulties as a result of his many languages.

If and when real problems do occur (the child does not speak a single word in *any* language before three), is "behind" in many milestones (speaking, sitting, walking, physical coordination, holding a spoon on his own, etc.), or shows signs of deafness (this can easily be tested by whispering behind the child's head that you'd like to give him a bar of chocolate, could he please turn around?), specialists should be consulted.

It is always a blessing when you can trust your child's doctor. However, if you do not feel that she is evaluating your child's situation properly, do not hesitate to seek out a second opinion. I have a friend who thought her son had a language problem. He did not speak clearly though he was six years old, and she thought he was getting worse instead of improving. She was convinced it was due to the many languages that surrounded him in their international community and that his problem was related to his multilingualism. She was about to give up the idea of a multilingual family. Then one day in a fit of frustration she yelled at him, "What are you, deaf or something!" In that same moment she bit her lip, took the boy to the doctor and found that his entire left ear canal was immersed in a soupy liquid which had caused his inability to hear. This had been caused by a "flat" ear canal, not by his multilingual upbringing. Over several months this had caused his increasing "deafness" and his own slurring of words as he could not hear himself speak. In very few cases is multilingualism the culprit. It is a very easy target, however, as research in the field is so slim and the amount of "evidence" in the negative camp is so great, as we saw earlier.

Four very helpful books, Janet Lees and Shelagh Urwin's (1996) *Children With Language Disorders*, Pamela Grunwell's (1995) *Developmental Speech Disorders*, James Law's (1992) *The Early Indentification of Language Impairment in Children*, and Smiley and Goldstein's (1998) *Language Delays and Disorders: From Research to Practice*, clearly identify the areas of real concern. If you suspect your child has either age-related problems (does not have language skills on par with others his age) or skill-related problems (certain language skills should parallel each other, like symbolic language understanding and expressive language, for example), a variety of tests are available to evaluate him. These tests cover all the areas of speech known to date and include the following for young children: *auditory reception* (can he hear well?); *visual reception* (can he see well?); *auditory association* (does he know that a dog has hair and a fish has ____?); *visual association* (can he match the bird with the nest and the bear with the cave?); *manual expression* (can he show you what a hammer or fork is used for?); and *verbal expression* (can he tell you a story?). In your child's verbal expression there are sub-categories to consider as well. This means examining whether or not *vocabulary, sentence structure, word choice*, and *grammar* are at age level. And remember that, as Pinker pointed out in an earlier chapter, "age level" is also a term which can vary greatly, sometimes as much as twelve months in either direction.

With the aid of these and other such language evaluations, however, parents are often reassured that their child does indeed fall within the "normal" range of development. Of course it is always better to be safe than sorry and a parent's hunch about her child's abilities should be pursued clinically for peace of mind.

Remember, however, as we mentioned earlier, bilinguals do tend to speak slightly later than monolinguals, just as boys speak slightly later than girls and subsequent children slightly later than first-borns. Parents with grown children as well as the research in the field can attest to the fact that some time around grade school, however, everyone's abilities even out. Parents of multilinguals have an "extra job" on top of all the other normal concerns of raising children. That is to be sure not to fall into the old trap of blaming their child's multiple languages on developmental problems. In most situations this just is not the case. It is increasingly clear that multiple languages add to the child's mental flexibility, do not impair the mind, or burden it.

Some books I have found helpful in specific areas are listed below by category and are recommended to the reader.

SOME SUGGESTED READINGS

Books about Bilingual Families

* *The Bilingual Family: A Handbook For Parents*, by Edith Harding and Philip Riley, Cambridge University Press, Great Britain, ninth printing 1996.
* *A Parents and Teachers Guide to Biligualism*, by Colin Baker, 2nd edition, Multiligual Matters, England, 2000.
* *Raising Children Bilingually: The Pre-School Years*, by Lenore Arnberg, Multilingual Matters, England, 1987.
* *A Guide to Family Reading in Two Languages—The Preschool Years*, by Theodore Andersson, National Clearinghouse for Bilingual Education, Virginia, 1981.
* *The Third Culture Kid Experience: Growing Up Among Worlds*, by David Pollock and Ruth E. Van Reken, Intercultural Press, Maine, 1999.

Books about Reading and Bilingual Children

* *Writing in a Bilingual Program: Había Una Vez*, by Carole Edelsky, Arizona State University, Ablex Publishing Co., New Jersey, 1986.
* *Reading and the Bilingual Child*, by Doris Ching, a reading aids series, California State University at Los Angeles, International Reading Association, Newark, Delaware, 1976.
* *Bilingual Performance in Reading and Writing*, by Alister Cumming (editor), John Benjamin's Publishing Company, Ann Arbor, Michigan, 1994.
* *Reading in the Bilingual Classroom: Literacy and Biliteracy*, by Kenneth Goodman, Yetta Goodman, and Barbara Flores, National Clearinghouse for Bilingual Education, Virginia, 1984.
* *Learning to Read in Different Languages*, Linguistic and Literacy Series: 1, by Sarah Hudelson (editor), Center for Applied Linguistics, Roger W. Shuy, General Series Editor, Washington DC, 1981.
* *Teaching Reading to Bilingual Children Study*, Vols.1–6, Document BRS-84-R, 1-I, 6, by Robert C. Calfee, Betty J. Mace-Matluck, and Wesley A. Hoover, Southwest Educational Developmental Laboratory, Texas, November, 1984.

Books about Multilingualism and Schools

- *Critical Reflection and the Foreign Language Classroom*, by Terry Osborn, Bergin and Garvey, Westport, Connecticut, 2000.
- *Languages and Children: Making the Match*, by H. Curtain and C. Pesola, Longman, New York, 1994.
- *Multiculture et Education en Europe*, by Cristina Allemann-Ghionda, Peter Lang, Bern, Switzerland, 1997.
- *European Models of Bilingual Education*, by Hugo Baetens Beardsmore (editor), Multilingual Matters, Ltd., England, 1993.
- *Educating Language Minority Children*, by Diane August and Kenji Hakuta (editors), National Academy Press, New York, 1998.
- *Mirror of Language: The Debate on Bilingualism*, by Kenji Hakuta, Basic Books, Inc., New York, 1986.
- *The Development of Second Language Proficiency*, by Birgit Harley, Patrick Allen, Jim Cummins, Merrill Swain (editors), Cambridge Applied Linguistic Series, Michael H. Long and Jack C. Richards Series Editors, Cambridge University Press, 1990.
- *Second-Language Acquisition in Childhood, Vol. 2: School Age Children*, by Barry McLaughlin, Lawrence Erlbaum Associates Publishers, New Jersey, 1985.

Books about Brain Research and Multilingualism

- *Pathways to the Brain: The Neurocognitive Basis of Language*, by Sydney M. Lamb, John Benjamins Publisher, Amsterdam, 1999.
- *Aspects of Bilingual Aphasia*, by Michel Paradis, Pergamon Press, 1995.
- *The Neurobiology of Affect in Language*, by John Schumann, Blackwell Publishers, Language Learning Research Club, University of Michigan, 1997.
- *The Crosslinguistic Study of Language Acquisition*, by Dan Isaac Slobin (editor), vols. 1–2, Lawrence Erlbaum Associates Publishers, New Jersey, 1992.
- *Language Processing in Bilingual Children*, by Ellen Bialystok, Cambridge University Press, England, 1991.
- *An Invitation to Cognitive Science: Language Vol. I*, edited by Lila R. Gleitman and Mark Liberman, general series editor, Daniel N. Osherson, a Bradford Book, The MIT Press, Cambridge, Massachusetts, 1995.
- *The Bilingual Brain: Neuropsychological and Neurolinguistic Aspects of Bilingualism*, by M. L. Albert and L. Obler, Academia Press, New York, 1979.

- *Readings on Aphasia in Bilinguals and Polyglots*, by Michel Paradis (editor), Didier, Canada, 1983.
- *Left Brain, Right Brain*, by Sally Springer and Georg Deutsch, W. H. Freeman and Company, New York, 1989.

Some Tests of Language Development for Children to Determine the Origins of Delayed Speech

- The Symbolic Play Test (Low and Costello 1976)
- Renfrew Tests (Renfrew 1972)
- Test For Reception of Grammar (Bishop 1983)
- The Boehms Test of Basic Concepts (Boehms 1986)
- The Bracken Basic Concept Scale (Bracken 1984)
- Carrow Elicited Language Inventory (1974)
- The Test of Word Finding (German 1986)
- The Reynell Developmental Language Scales (Revised 1987)
- Porch Index of Communicative Ability in Children (Porch 1970)
- Illinois Test of Psycholinguistic Abilities (Kirk, McCarthy, and Kirk 1968)
- Clinical Evaluation of Language Functions (Semel and Wiig 1987)
- The Ashton Index: A screening procedure for written language difficulties (Newton and Thompson 1976)

Source: Lees and Urwin, *Children with Language Disorders*, Whurr Publishers, London, 1996.

Now that it is clearer what situations are related to actual language developmental problems, and which can be attributed to other causes, let us look closer at a common concern of many families. What can be done if parents realize they have approached their child's foreign language development in a less-than-optimal way? How and when can families change language strategies to contribute to a solution rather than compound the problem? This is what we turn to in the last section in this chapter.

CHANGING LANGUAGE STRATEGIES

A Successful Snapshot to Get the Big Picture

Clara is a very loving, concerned working mother. Her son is in the French school, her husband is British, Clara is Portuguese, and they have a live-in house cleaner who is also Portuguese. All of her son's life she has spoken to him in English because she felt "it was a more useful language than Portuguese." Last year she began to regret it. Thomas was five-and-a-half years old and spoke French and English fluently, but did not speak a word of Portuguese. On a family holiday to visit Clara's parents and other relatives it became clear that Thomas could not function in that language, and this was a painful realization for the family. Clara wanted to know what to do. Was it too late? Wouldn't Thomas be confused if she switched languages on him after five-and-a-half years? How could they go about "rescuing" the chance at her native language?

At this time Thomas was in the Second Window, a perfect time for an already bilingual child to learn a third language. French and Portuguese are very closely related languages linguistically. And Thomas had a passive knowledge of Portuguese having heard it from birth, though not in conversation directed towards him. We worked on a new family strategy which included Thomas' agreement. Once beyond five years old, children (with a few exceptions) have a cognitive understanding of their language(s). They know who speaks their language(s) and what to call each one. Using this knowledge, Clara approached Thomas on a very cerebral, reasoning level using emotional motivation to discuss switching language strategies on him. Clara asked Thomas if he liked traveling to Portugal. Yes. Wasn't it fun visiting with your cousins and eating at grandma's house? Yes. Did you know Mommy's first language is Portuguese? Yes. Would you like to learn to speak in Portuguese too? Yes.

At that moment she began to speak to Thomas exclusively in Portuguese. His father continued to speak only in English, and the parents continued to speak English to each other. She said that after just two short weeks, Thomas began speaking back to her in brief phrases. She said when he spoke his first words in Portuguese it was like hearing an infant say "mama" for the first time. She cried. Two months after the change she said Thomas no longer doubted whether to speak to her in Portuguese or English, he always did so in Portuguese. A year later Clara reported that his Portuguese was nearly as fluent as his English.

While Clara and Thomas' case lent itself extremely well to such a strategy change, other families may not have the advantage of having the languages linguistically related, or the cooperation of the child who in this case saw clear benefits to learning the new language.

Three steps must be taken if and when parents decide to change strategies on a child:

1. Get the child's agreement for change;
2. Decide on the new strategy together;
3. Be consistent in the new strategy and do not change anything not agreed upon by the family as a whole.

Once a child is in the Second Window, the extremely important role of Motivation must be used to favorably instigate change. In this case, Clara spoke to Thomas about the fond memories he had while visiting his family abroad. In your own case it may be to talk about how wonderful the new teacher is, and wouldn't it be great to be able to communicate in her language? The important thing to remember is that children, even small babies, rely on consistency in communication with you. Remember my son Gabriel and our mistaken language switch which I feel was directly responsible for his slowness to speak? This means that if and when a strategy change is undertaken it is consistent and/or consciously accepted by the child. Such a change can only take place when a child is "cognitively mature," that is, has the brain space to deal with such concepts as "different languages" and has stopped mixing languages. In some particularly mature children, this can be as young as four-and-a-half, and it is probably safe to say that most six-year-olds can handle a conscious change of strategy. Your role as the parent and language strategist is crucial here, and you must realize that your child relies on you for a clear decision in this area if and when a change is to take place.

Hopefully with the information presented in this book, fewer and fewer family cases will have to be "repaired" and more and more families will enjoy the rewards of raising multilingual children. Now for some concluding ideas.

_____ *Chapter 10* _____

The Sweet Smell of Success

A SUMMARY

By keeping a check-list in mind of the ingredients that make up your child's smorgasbord of language possibilities you will be able to track your family's progress towards multilingualism. By understanding which Window your child is in, you know when great things can be expected (always in the First Window, for example), and when there are less active times for new language learning (two to four years old). And you can better sympathize with the hardships your ten-year-old must face learning a new language compared with his younger five-year-old sister. Aptitude is the second of our two ingredients. Children are born with a certain level of aptitude which, if high, can be used to enhance their foreign language learning. While your influence on your child's aptitude is limited to what you have given him through your genes, you now know how to identify it and work to enhance whatever level he does have.

Under *Baking Instructions* we spoke about the importance of motivation, strategy, and consistency. With the role of motivation clear, you can be sure to fulfill your role in encouraging your child's efforts and be sure to model the behavior you hope to solicit. The great importance of consciously choosing a family language strategy and being consistent with it are also factors every family must incorporate into their own child's recipe.

Under *Kitchen Design* (the Language Learning Environment) the roles of Opportunity, the Linguistic Relationship Between Languages, and how Siblings can effect language learning were covered. By noting what opportunities are available within the home, school, and community, families can make the most of their surroundings when it comes to language learning. While children who learn their languages in the First Window do not have to be concerned about the linguistic relationship between their languages, as no language is easier or harder to learn to a newborn, families with children learning languages after this stage need to be aware of the similarities or differences in the linguistic roots of the languages. Understanding if and how your child's first language is related to a potential second language can influence your decision to take on the new language. For example, families being posted abroad can evaluate the language of their host countries with English and determine whether or not there is a favorable linguistic relationship. With regard to siblings, we noted that while there are both potential benefits as well as drawbacks to siblings' influences over each other's language development, in the great majority of cases parents can be assured that having a brother or sister helps a child in learning a foreign language.

In *Plumbing and Electricity* (the Multilingual Brain) the possible importance of Gender and Hand Use were studied, and the overall concept of how our multilingual children's brains are structured was explained. It was noted that boys generally begin life less verbal than their female counterparts and remain so throughout their lives. However, this does not mean that boys are any worse at learning foreign languages than girls. It does mean, rather, that it may be necessary to give boys more time to show their language talents than girls. Within the area of Hand Use we spoke of the different abilities associated with the left and right hemispheres of the brain and how multilingual children may have enhanced skills due to where foreign languages are located cerebrally.

In *The Chefs and Chefs' Assistants* we went into depth about the role of Teachers and Schools in a child's foreign language learning endeavor. The often primary role of teachers in your child's foreign language endeavors was discussed and many teaching strategies provided. While you may not be able to chose the school your child attends, there are specific things you can look for in a teacher and a classroom setting. When they are missing you know what will need shoring up at home.

In *Baking Your Own*, each family was asked to undertake a serious self-evaluation in terms of foreign language learning. Parents were then asked to complete their own Family Language Profile to see how the ten factors fit into their own case, and then to evaluate their own Family Language Goals. If the decided goals included Multiliteracy Skills, parents were asked to read that section carefully and to understand that it is indeed a challenge, but one well worth the effort, if chosen.

In *A Mess in the Kitchen* we took a hard look at what problem situations may exist, and when such problems are rightly or wrongly attributed to a child having multiple languages. The history of how polyglots have been perceived in society was reviewed, hinting at why it has been easy up until recently to blame many language problems on a child's multilingualism. A list of suggested readings followed.

Finally, I would now like to conclude with some diary entries about my own children's language development challenges and successes in order to more fully illustrate the material in this book.

A DIARY ACCOUNT OF MY CHILDREN'S LANGUAGE DEVELOPMENT

In this section, as a parent-cum-linguist, I include some notes from my own three children's language development.

Diary Notes about Natalie, Gabriel, and Mateo (July 1996 Quito)

Beginning Life Bilingual

This is Natalie's story, and Gabriel's, and in the developmental spirit, to their unborn brother who is coming along in eight months' time. It is mostly about Natalie, as she is the oldest, and my concerns about language sprang from her birth three years and four months ago.

Natalie was "made in Japan" while my husband, Cristian, served in the Ecuadorian Diplomatic Mission and I taught at the International School of the Sacred Heart in Tokyo. She was born in Quito, Ecuador, on December 4, 1992 at 9:33 a.m. into the hands of enthusiastic, Spanish-speaking doctors telling stories about the bull–fighting season which was at its height the day she came into the world during the *Fiestas de Quito.* At thirteen months we took Natalie to Geneva, Switzerland, for four months as my husband was sent on a special course at the United Nations. So just as she was learning to speak her first words in English and Spanish, she was faced with playground confrontations, shopping expeditions, transportation, and elevator music all in French rhythm, syntax, and energy, different from what she had experienced before. She began to attend a play-school in Quito at twenty-two months. She understood nearly everything said to her in both English or Spanish and had a working spoken vocabulary of exactly 100 words in English and nine in Spanish (I kept a list for my linguistically interested mother who never failed to ask in earnest "so what is Natalie saying these days?"). Her English vocabulary superiority was due to the fact that before entering day care she spent twenty-four hours a day in my company, and I spoke to her exclusively in English by design. This one-person, one-language strategy seemed the most logical approach to us at the time. Once in school in Quito her Spanish quickly improved and within six months her vocabulary was evenly split between English and Spanish. At two-and-a-half she began mixing Spanish and English words, inserting vocabulary from one language or another when she didn't know the word in the second language. I must say I believe she maintained relatively good grammatical structure—that is, if she began the sentence in English, she kept the syntax, only inserting Spanish words when at a loss for their equivalent, as in proper names or titles. This lasted for about six months. Just before three, Natalie was more or less clear about who spoke in which language. She only spoke English to me, only Spanish to her father, and clearly identified which language went with which person. This is the same age at which Hildegard Werner separated her languages (Werner Leopold 1939–1949). On the telephone she would speak to her American grandparents in English without hesitation, and in the next breath look to her Spanish-speaking grandmother and chatter in Spanish.

A Change in Language Strategies (August 1996, Boston)

When Natalie turned three-and-a-half and when her younger brother was thirteen months old we moved from Quito to Boston, Massachusetts, where my husband began a year-long program of studies at Harvard University. We have been here now two months. She adores the new school, and her English sophistication is flourishing among encouraging teachers and bright peers. But we have one problem with Gabriel now. We have changed language strategies.

To preserve Spanish, we decided that as a family we would supposedly speak Spanish to each other, and let the English take care of itself as it is all around us in the environment. I say supposedly as this is extremely difficult for me, as I am the one who has to switch and begin speaking to my children in Spanish, something I consciously fought not to do the whole time I was in Ecuador. Gabriel turned one at the end of May, and we moved June 21, 1996. Because of his personality he doesn't seem to speak much. It seems to me that he spends all of his brain power on learning to master gross motor skills like walking, throwing, bouncing, and banging, and little if any energy on speaking. He is so very different from Natalie. Though both children have experienced a change of country and language at thirteen months (Natalie when we went to Geneva and Gabriel now), Natalie's language abilities seemed to blossom due to the stimulation while Gabriel's have frozen. He is making extremely slow advances with respect to new vocabulary and general social skills, but great leaps physically, running and climbing almost as he learned to walk, things his sister did not dare to attempt. Is this because he is a boy? A second child? A second child in a bilingual family that had just changed language strategies on him? Yes on all counts, his pediatrician at Harvard said to us last week. Add to those three factors a fourth, she said, which was an overly helpful sister who translated his every need into a clear verbal request. The end result, Gabriel speaks little in either English or Spanish. I hope I can find some other encouraging information when I begin my classes next week.

Adding a Third Language (February 1997, Boston)

In January 1997 we had to decide on a school for Natalie for the following academic year when we would return to Ecuador. All five school options had deadlines at this time, and so, long-distance, we chose my husband's alma mater, the German School of Quito. In the winter of 1997 when Natalie was four years, one month old and Gabriel was twenty-one months they began going to a German caregiver's house two afternoons a week. Ute and her five-year-old daughter, Hjordes, were asked to speak exclusively in German to the children.

"I learned something funny, mommy!" says Natalie with a look of glee when I picked her up from Ute and Hjordes' house late one March afternoon. "You know how you say 'hot' in German? *Heiss*! Like *ice* in English, isn't that silly?!" This has been Natalie's approach to learning vocabulary ever since I can remember. Everything is a game, everything is funny. It all seems rooted in previous language skills, the humor coming from the relation of the words from different countries. Gabriel, on the other hand, simply incorporates vocabulary, giving little or no relation to other words, as is typical for his age, I guess. He got on the phone with his English-speaking grandmother while he was holding an "egg mobile" made of blown egg shells that they had made at Ute's house. He tells grandma, "hello, hi *ei, ei, ei* [pointing to the mobile], bye bye!" "*Ei*" is the German word for egg. (What kind of "wiring" is there that he automatically connects the words by sound, rhyming "hi," "*ei*," and "bye" into his single sentence, though in two languages? I'll have to ask the neurology professor.) When Gabriel is prompted to say goodbye to someone he usually responds these days by saying, "*Bye–Ciao-Tschüss*" and waving. One language and no conscious separation. He sees all of these words as fitting into a single system. Gabriel is treating all words as part of "his" singular language system, whereas Natalie now knows that there is such a thing as different languages and that not everyone speaks the same language, nor understands what she understands.

But she has always been a little special in that regard. Natalie actually separated languages to an extreme. After recognizing at around three that "mommy speaks English and daddy speaks Spanish," she then invented her own language which she often spoke with "Matoman," her imaginary playmate. I suppose, like twins who develop their own communication system, Natalie had assumed that if mommy had a language and daddy had one, then perhaps everyone had their own, and she had to make hers up. She would often sing the tune of a familiar song, but with invented words. "*Row Row Row Your Boat*" would come out "*Isa Isa Isa Tooo*," all making perfect sense in her own head. I see something similar in Gabriel, rhythmically related. He has, like many twenty-one month olds, the rhythm of the language, the intonation, and the facial expressions that accompany conversation, but he doesn't have the words, he just has a series of inconsistent sounds that accompany his exchange with others. At this point he speaks just thirty words in English, six in Spanish, and three in

German, (*Tschüss, Ei, Schuh*) though it is obvious he understands most everything in Spanish and English. He takes a bite of food and looks at me inquisitively, smiling a little, "doo ooh?" which is something like, "is it good?" or "is it delicious?" which *I* usually ask *him* over meals. If I answer, "yes, delicious," he smiles in pure satisfaction that we have just had a conversation that he has initiated.

Losing and then Recovering a Language (March 1997)

We have been in Boston nine months now. Natalie is four years, three months old and she mainly speaks to Cristian and me in English these days, having slowly stopped speaking to her father in Spanish over the last four months. However, I noticed last Sunday that she initiated playing with two other Ecuadorians (ages seven and eight) in Spanish. She hesitated at first, asking me how to say "look for" (*buscar*) in Spanish. When I told her she quickly recovered the rhythm of the exchange and began to speak in Spanish. She spent the next few hours at play with them, all in Spanish and without hesitation, confirming my belief that she will once again speak to her father and friends in Quito in Spanish with just a little prompting and time. If you don't use it, you lose it, I suppose. Having not had Spanish around her as consistently as she did in Quito, and not having a large number of Spanish-speaking friends here, makes it hard for her to find the language's rhythm, but find it she does.

I remember while taking Japanese classes in Tokyo I asked the young language instructor if I might be able to listen to the chapter cassette ahead of time, as it helped me with the rhythm of the language. She looked at me as if I were a little crazy and asked me to explain "rhythm." My fellow classmates jumped in and supported me in trying to explain why it was so important to understand the highs and lows of the sentences, the intonation of the speakers, with subtle differences between men and women speakers in conversation, the pauses and fillers "*uhhh, neh, sooo.*" To my distress the teacher never understood the request. Having watched Gabriel these days I find such rhythm so basic in his beginning abilities to communicate. His voice rises with a questioning blurb, his eyebrows gather and his voice deepens when he reprimands a doll in his fictitious tongue, all so important to understanding the exchange, even if the actual words fail him.

Continuing Natalie's Story (July 31, 1998, Geneva)

Between July and November 1997 we returned to Ecuador from Boston before moving to Switzerland. As expected, Natalie's Spanish returned after just a few days of being in the language environment. Gabriel continued to speak only minimally in either language. Mateo, our third child, was just seven months old when we moved to a suburb of French-speaking Geneva.

After our move from Boston to Quito briefly, and now to Geneva, we have settled into a routine and Natalie has a school. At this point, Natalie has attended the German School here from December 1, 1997 to June 1998, and is currently on vacation until August 26, 1998. While her first two months proved a kind of honeymoon period, she went through a difficult time beginning the first week of February 1998 (at five years and two months) when she regularly wet her bed at night and began crying and nearly panicking when left at school in the morning. The teacher was very supportive and acknowledged that there must be something going on in Natalie's life, but could it have to do with her new younger brother? While at school she was the happiest kid and enjoyed herself tremendously, volunteering constantly to do things for the teacher, sing songs, answer questions (but sometimes timidly lowering her arm, because she understood what was being asked, but sometimes couldn't find the words to answer). Cristian and I discarded the brother theory offered by the teacher simply because we couldn't find anything to support it at home, and the timing of her bedwetting episodes was directly correlated to school. When on school holiday over Easter she did not have night wetting. When school commenced again it usually would occur on Sunday night, but almost never on Friday or Saturday night, or more clearly stated, only when there was school the next morning. It did not occur at all while on vacation for two weeks from the end of May until June 12th in California and Hawaii. This continued for several weeks and still happened occasionally here and there in June 1998, but has completely disappeared since school let out on June 20th. After speaking with her pediatrician, we came to the conclusion that it most definitely is language pressure which is causing her stress. Outwardly she remained very lively and happy and talked positively about what went on at school, but apparently she was troubled by some of the children who wanted "to play alone" during recess, meaning without her, and others who actually roughed her up during recess in a "game" which scared her thoroughly. Her very social nature and strong personality were beneficial in some cases and detrimental in others. She was very willing to be with all kinds of children, but she had a difficult time being alone, and sometimes the language barrier isolated her. During vacation, however, she has taken great pride in being able to "translate" for Mom and her brothers on a short trip to Freiburg in Germany, and is very pleased that I will start German classes next Monday. She had asked to take a French class this summer because she "was behind" the neighborhood kids, but Cristian felt it wiser to let her settle completely into the German program before piling on the French. We have compromised with a week-long workshop she will attend with Gabriel at his old crèche, which is in English and French together. Natalie says she is very pleased that I will now also be able to help her with reading her German books at story-time at night, and that she can help me with my homework, talk to the teachers, and maybe even come on some of the field trips like the other mommies who help out at school, "especially since Gabriel will be starting school too and might need more help" than she did. Her level of German is good given the short amount of time she has been in the environment, says her teacher, and this is one reason she discounted Natalie's bedwetting as related to school stress. Her doctor, who is originally from Japan but who studied in Switzerland and who speaks Japanese, French, Spanish, and English thoroughly believes Natalie is stressed due to the language challenges as well as the larger change of country and home. I tend to agree. We have been here just six months and our house is just now becoming "settled." Apparently, Natalie's teacher says that she is far more concerned about other kids in her class who have German parents but refuse to speak German, than about Natalie who tries constantly, even beyond her capabilities. It seems like this "tough cookie" personality, her strength of character, is helping her with her language acquisition, even if the school environment in terms of friends is less than optimal.

Gabriel, on the other hand, has come into his own. He is now three years and nearly two months old. He speaks much more now, not reaching Natalie's constant narrative level, but now interrupting her to yell, "Nati, it's my turn, my turn! Now!" and also tries to give answers and explanations and opinions. In the car on the ride home from school I ask them about their days and Gabriel will answer if prodded, a step in the right direction, at least. I think Mateo, who is now fifteen months old, has been a bit of an inspiration to Gabriel, and visa versa. He speaks (albeit in a limited fashion) without prompting. Upon leaving the play area at the local *Chavannes Centre* mall, I told the children to say "*merci, au revoir*" to the woman who tends the center. Mateo said "*au revoir!*" and waved before the other two could open their mouths, causing us all to laugh and Gabriel to follow suit, "*merci! au revoir!*" in a flood of laughter.

A Quiet, Concentrated Sibling, But Slow to Speak?

Gabriel's understanding and use of English is on par with others his age, according to his pediatrician, and she understands his speech (which I was worried about being delayed), though he doesn't volunteer much information. While in California and Hawaii in May–June he was showered with compliments about how well he spoke, how handsome he was, and what a good boy he seemed to be. (I wonder what they would say if they had him for a twenty-four hour stretch!?) In any case, this trip was so good for his ego. Every day he was told he was great by a lot of people who loved him. What more can you ask? He came back to Switzerland, leaving diapers behind (except at night), speaking more clearly and boasting several skills before undiscovered, like his keen sense of observation (enjoys *Where's Waldo* books enormously), ability with puzzles (loves the geometric-shape book his Aunt Amie gave him), and long concentration span, which I guess we had seen much earlier in life, but which I never appreciated before I had to ride on an airplane for eleven hours with him (Zurich to San Francisco). At one point he sat for over an hour-and-a-half coloring and looking at the pages of his *Barney* book. In that same time period Natalie had gone to the bathroom twice, pulled out her books, played cards, asked for a snack, and tried all the stations on the headset. (What does this say about Gabriel's brain? Strong concentration and analytical skills, low verbal and social. . . . Is this a typical right-handed male?!) While his English has flourished and his Spanish comprehension has increased, his Spanish speaking has not made equal progress. He understands everything, it seems, but generally refuses to use it. He will tell Cristian "not *manzana*, it's an apple!" and they go back and forth repeating the words and laughing about it, but for whatever reason, he chooses not to use Spanish. I am hoping that when his godmother (who is seventeen years old) and his grandmother (*Abuelita* Ana) come for a visit next week he will feel more inspired. He has had a lot to cope with for a little three-year-old: his focus on the bathroom routine, dressing himself, being an older brother, speaking English, settling into this environment . . . I guess I can wait a few more months for the Spanish to kick in, though I hope he starts to use it soon. There is a pretty strong chance we will not go to Quito for Christmas this year, meaning he will have no Spanish influence except for Cristian and our embassy friends and infrequent guests for quite a long time.

I have read a lot of things about bilingual children who refuse to speak in one of their languages. What are the possible causes? Of those I can recall, one had to do with refusing to compete with an older sibling. Could it be that Gabriel does not speak much in Spanish because he does not want to compete with the ever-talkative Natalie on that level? Another reason had to do with being "overly sensitive" to those around him, that is, if he knows that there is someone present who is not speaking that language (me, for example; I speak with my husband in English at home), then the child doesn't speak in the "foreign" tongue (in this case Spanish) out of courtesy, though I'm not sure Gabriel's that polite. . . . Then there's the idea of "receptive only bilinguals," which could very well be Gabriel's case. In this scenario, the child is a far better listener than speaker, comprehends but doesn't express himself. I suppose time will tell.

Gabriel begins at the German School at the end of August 1998. We shared our concerns about his language progress with the pediatrician who asked immediately if we felt he was competent in at least one language. I told her yes, in English, and that he understands everything in Spanish, and some German phrases and words and something similar in French. She told me that if he had at least one language, she would not worry about it, because from her perspective, if he had the tools (language) to be able to *think* in at least one language then she wouldn't be concerned (Skutnabb-Kangas, 1976, also came to similar conclusions). However, she said, we should definitely keep the door open for a change in schools in September if we realize that he is undergoing an inordinate amount of stress. According to her, many kids have a hard time starting school to begin with, let alone in another language, and children from the same families can have a wide variety of aptitudes related to second language acquisition and we should not expect that he speak a second or third language as easily as his older sister.

A Third Child: A Third Combination of Strengths and Weaknesses

As for Mateo, Cristian and I have noted that he seems more similar to Natalie than to Gabriel in terms of developmental stages. He is now fifteen months old. He is a real talker and falls asleep at night babbling. He jumps into conversations with his gibberish, and he clearly communicates all his needs with a mish-mash of "words" and gestures. He's a dancer like his sister, loves a good hug, and gives kisses affectionately. He warms to people quickly and was a real show-off at my cousin's wedding because he got along with everyone, blowing kisses to all and smiling up a storm. He and Gabriel are going to get along tremendously well together, too. He tries desperately to keep up with Gabriel in all activities, though sometimes it's frustrating for them both. The other day at lunch Gabriel did not pay enough attention to Mateo, so Mateo stole Gabriel's straw from him and ran around the kitchen table squealing. Mateo spends a great deal of time "reading books" as do the other two. Before going to sleep they go to the shelves to choose a book, and Mateo goes right along with the other two, pulls out a book and thumbs through the pages. As mentioned earlier, Gabriel speaks a lot to Mateo, which is great for both of them. Gabriel will often tell Mateo "don't drink the water" in the bathtub, or "stop making lots of noise" in the car as *he* has been asked before. This exchange has been invaluable for Mateo in terms of his speech development. His intonation is perfect, though his exact words may be lacking. This is six months earlier than Gabriel was at this stage.

A Blossoming of Vocabulary (August 29, 1998, Geneva)

Mateo's vocabulary has blossomed, as has Gabriel's and Natalie's to a lesser extent, as is natural for vocabulary curves at their respective ages. Mateo is sixteen and a half months old and communicates well with a set of words in four languages: Mama, *maman* (French), mommy, papa, Ana, ma (*más*/more), juice, "chee" (cheese), *água*, Nannie and Annie (Natalie and Gabriel), *hola, au revoir*, "shasha" (*grácias*/ thank you), horse, "birrr(d)" (for all other animals), shoes, *bravo!*, pee-pee, ball (for all round objects including fruits); nose, eye, baaahh (bath), "dis" (this), "uppa" (lift me up) and the ever popular "no" and the ever present "me" and "mine!" He makes noises for cats, dogs, cows and horses. He follows all instructions in English and Spanish with equal fluency. He blows his nose upon command, finds his shoes when they are missing, drinks his juice or milk when asked, tells you what he wants to eat (along with running to the refrigerator or pulling the cereal box off the shelf), and lets you know when he has to "poo

poo" or "peepee." When asked if he is strong in either language (Are you strong?/*Tú eres fuerte?*) he flexes his arms and makes a fist "like Hercules," according to his sister, and makes a grunting noise as an affirmative response. All commands are responded to with nearly equal fluency in English or Spanish. He is a lively dancer and will often plant his feet firmly in one place and roll back and forth from the hips, sometimes in such a rhythm that he looks like a blind musician swaying to the tunes. He likes *salsa* and classical, rock, and children's music with equal *gusto*.

Gabriel is three years, three months, three days old and began school last Wednesday at the German School. Since his third birthday he has really increased his vocabulary accumulation, and whereas he has always had the proper intonation of a conversation (rising voice at the end of a question, etc.) he now finally has the words to match. After just three days of school I see a noticeable improvement in his pronunciation and clarity in *English*, though school instruction is in German. I suppose with the necessity to make himself clear, and without the ever present translator (his sister) to interpret his needs, he has now come to see the need to express himself better. His temperament has and I fear will keep him from leaping into the German language as Natalie did, as she is a real social being and lives for companionship, and he is not. Gabriel is happy playing on his own with a train set on the floor or creating a parade of animals from the drawer of puppets and does not crave playmates to have fun. He loves a good game of chase or monster, though, and growling is growling in any tongue, I suppose. He pays very definite attention to the stories read to him in any language, and (hopefully) the vocabulary differences. He loves books. Up to now he still responds in English ninety percent of the time, no matter in what language he is addressed in. In the *garderie* at the local shopping center where he and Natalie often play while I shop, I will tell the children to say goodbye when we are about to leave, and he does just that, "good bye" in English. When I tell him no, in French, he then says *"merci, au revoir,"* but only after being told in what language to use. On the plus side, he knows which words fit into which language category, on the down side he has to be told which language to speak. This is a big change from even just a month ago when he still did not distinguish in which language he spoke. Natalie, while often lacking vocabulary, is always clear about the language context on the other hand.

Gabriel will attend the German School in the mornings, usually from 8:30 a.m. until 12:20 p.m., so he will have about three-and-a-half hours of German daily. In addition, we are hoping to engage a university student or tutor to watch the children two afternoons a week who will only speak German to them. Gabriel's comprehension is complete in English and Spanish however. To a surprising extent his German understanding is also very good. When his teacher asked him the first day if these were his supplies (pencils, erasers, etc.), he responded "yes." Then she asked him to open the pencil sharpener and take it out of the wrapper (in German), and he did so without hesitation. After he chose a cubby (a clown/jester figure) she asked him if he had picked one, he nodded (did not say "yes" nor "*ja*") and pointed to his drawer. I don't know if he completely understood, or if her intonation with questions was just so good, or if the tasks were just so obvious, but I was surprised he followed all her instructions. There are two other children in the class of ten who have parents who speak to them in English, but I believe that all the children except Gabriel speak German at age-appropriate levels. This should be a factor forcing him to speak German quickly I believe, and after the first few weeks I think his teacher will not speak in English to him at all. She responds to his English requests in German, and sometimes repeats the answer in English if necessary.

Natalie started off this school year successfully. She says she loves her class, even though there are just four girls and ten boys in it. One of the girls is a tomboy and never plays with the other girls, and the other two girls have stuck together quite tightly. Natalie doesn't seem fazed outwardly for the moment. She was very proud that when the children were asked to identify their own names on a piece of paper that she was the first one to find hers, and that some of the others couldn't do it at all. She jumped right into the school situation in German, not using English as a crutch at all with the teachers who all have some knowledge of the language. She tries very hard to use all the vocabulary she has and constantly asks her father for words in German. She twisted her ankle the night before the second day of class, learned how to say "sprained ankle" in German, and then told everyone about her foot the next morning. Her challenge will now come at two other levels, I believe. She will have French two hours a week at school, adding a forth language formally. And she is starting to learn to read in English. So far she seems content, no bedwetting, and always stays happily when left off in the morning. Let the honeymoon last!

A Teacher's Input (October 11, 1998, Geneva)

We had meetings with both Gabriel's and Natalie's teachers last week to gauge their progress and adaptability over the past six weeks of school. My husband met with Natalie's teacher and learned a great deal about the classroom dynamics and its effect on her ability to make friends. Natalie is in the "princess stage," she loves to dress up, engage in imaginary play, etc. Unfortunately, there are only three other girls in her class, and the boys are "on the rough side." Of the three other girls, one is a tomboy and does not usually play with the girls. The other two have paired off in a rather closed clique and usually do not want Natalie to play with them, leaving her to either talk the boys into a game of house or go along with their games. Given her very social nature, this has made the classroom free time very hard for her. During structured activities she participates eagerly and works diligently, says her teacher. She also adores book time and follows the plot and story line with ease. Her vocabulary is at age level in German, though she often uses English grammar, says her teacher. We have had several of her classmates over to the house to play (four of the nine boys) and have one of the girls lined up for a visit after the fall break in two weeks' time. Hopefully we can cultivate some individual friendships on Natalie's turf which can ease her school time. Though she does not say so herself, not having a good school friend must be stressful. This stress in turn can make her feel negatively about school as a whole, which is her only source of German for the moment. On the lighter side, her German teacher says she notices that Natalie really enjoys her French period and is doing well there. She had originally tried to discourage us from enrolling her in the extra French classes because she felt it would be too much for Natalie. We convinced her that it would be one place in school where she would be on equal or better footing than her German counterparts, and a big boost for her ego. We were right.

Gabriel is very happy at school, though he says "I don't like" to speak in German, and usually responds to the teacher in English, if at all. He does, however, sing in German and follows most instructions. His teacher says he's "too smart for his own good," since he knows that she can speak English (which he has seen her do often at pick-up time), so he does not bother to speak in German. She also feels that he relies too much on Natalie during recess, for example, and does not have any need to push himself to learn. He has sought out two other children who speak English with whom he plays most of the time, or he happily plays by himself.

We have decided to engage a German woman recommended by the school who will come to our house twice a week in the afternoons to play with the children and supervise their school friends' visits. We will also try and have Gabriel do more activities with his own friends, rather than tagging along with Natalie. This should encourage his own language development.

Mateo is advancing greatly in terms of his first languages. He has added a host of proper names to his vocabulary (including Mickey Mouse and Ernie from *Sesame Street*). From nine months to one year old he sat in on my private French lessons. Now he accompanies me to German classes at the United Nations Women's Guild where I take a class with four other ladies. Sometimes he pretends to write notes, other times he sleeps or plays, but somehow I am sure he is "getting it." Upon leaving class yesterday he blew the ladies kisses and said, "*Tschüss!* Bye!" In the last six weeks he has added "pweeze" (please), "nanoh" (*hermano*), Ernie, Mickey, Barney, go, door, down, hair, mouth, knee, bottle, "der" (there), *ahí* (Spanish for over "there"), ball. All little girls seem to be "Ana" these days. He is doing a lot more screaming lately, with words and without (if it's with words it is usually "mine!" or "no!"). He continues to promise strong language skills, I feel.

Resigning Oneself to the Language (January 30, 1999)

Natalie is now six years, two months old. Gabriel is three years, eight months old, and Mateo is nearly twenty-two months old.

Well, we did get to Quito for Christmas, but it was a kind of mixed blessing. Whereas Gabriel and Mateo greatly improved their Spanish, Natalie became more conscious of how far away we live from the rest of the family. She was very sad the day we left Ecuador to return to Switzerland. On top of that, four days after our return and right before school was to begin, Natalie and Gabriel came down with chicken pox, keeping them out of the school pattern for another week. However, after regaining their health we planned a costume party to belatedly celebrate Natalie's birthday with her classmates. The party was a wonderful success. Twelve children from school (German-speakers) two neighbors (English-speakers) and two close family friends (Spanish-speakers) attended. The woman who tutors Natalie in German, Monika, and who has become a very good friend, devised several games and helped organize the children for a Treasure Hunt, the piñata, and "make your own" ice cream sundae. I think Natalie was genuinely pleased, though she spent a good deal of the party translating from German into Spanish or English. Right after her party she came down with another illness and consequently has missed two weeks in this month at school. Next week are the parent–teacher conferences so we can evaluate her academic and social progress better. She seems resigned to her classroom situation, not happy, but not depressed either. We are lucky she enjoys Monika's German classes so much; she has developed a strong positive bond to German through her games and careful choice of activities.

Gabriel's vocabulary is improving all around, thank goodness. His English sentences are smoother and he now takes pleasure in speaking Spanish, but usually only when prompted to speak by his father. He is also learning a lot of new words in German (whole songs, body parts, etc.). He has been in an exceptionally good mood ever since our trip to Quito. He tries hard to make people laugh, a real clown, and he's become very caring and gentle towards his younger brother, bringing him toys if he cries and making silly faces to cheer him up. He has become far more demonstrative in his affection for others. He openly hugs his friends at school and gives kisses with greater frequency. He is very happy at school and with his teacher. He does a lot of imaginary play lately, finding treasure chests full of diamonds (which he graciously gives to his mother), or cares for a baby koala in his arms by feeding it a "koala leaf." He is a real pleasure to be around.

Mateo is actually speaking in little sentences ("juice yes, book yes") and has added several words to his vocabulary: nose, eyes, teeth, tongue, head, toes, tummy, ears, neck, body, hand, baby, potty, book, milk. In Spanish every number is "*dos*" (two) and every food is "*papas*" (potatoes). He understands most colors and animals in Spanish and indicates them by pointing and sometimes repeating the names (*buho, gato, elefante*). He appears to have equal comprehension in English and Spanish.

None of the children seems to fuss if the afternoon cartoons are on in French or English or whether they watch *Peter Pan* in German or the *Dalmatians* in French. They have just accepted this as a part of how life is here.

A Spring and Summer of Visitors and Foreign Countries (April–August 1999)

What a wonderful spring and summer we have had! Between April and August we had nine sets of house guests which gave us a terrific opportunity to travel around Switzerland and other parts of Europe. When my mother came to Germany, the children got a chance to use their German a bit, and did so again when we went to visit some family friends near Frankfurt for a week. And while I was pleased at seeing them use German, I was intrigued with Natalie's fascination with Italian.

When my father came we went to Italy and, while we all thought it was wonderful for the food, people, and sights, Natalie was also drawn to the language. She wanted to listen to Andrea Bocelli's opera, said she understood the waiters, ordered her own food using a mixture of Italian and Spanish. Milan, Pisa, Florence, and Assisi were wonders in and of themselves, but having this little revelation was also fascinating. "If I know Italian, then I'll know the same languages as Cristina," she boasted. ("Cristina" is Dr. Allemann-Ghionda, a friend and professor at the university here who speaks precisely German, Spanish, English, French, and Italian).

And then we had a special visit from Cristian's brother and his family. We had a great time returning to Italy via Milan and then went to Germany and France's Strasbourg with them. So in the span of a few months we really chalked up the miles on the minivan, three times to Germany, twice to Italy, countless times across the border to France. Our central location has been key to using the foreign languages we are studying.

In between travels the children went to Monika's for German tutoring. They played with her kittens, baked bread, harvested cucumbers, and chased chickens, learning a greater variety of German vocabulary than they normally would at school, I think. Happily both children get on so well with her and have made such a strong, positive connection to the German language through her friendship.

The Amazing Minds of Children (September 17, 1999)

I cannot stop being happily in awe of the children's abilities to learn languages and to adjust. Natalie began first grade with a bang. She thinks she has the "best teacher in the world" and claims there is no math or reading or German or French lessons, only games—clever teacher! Her new teacher believes Natalie has very good German and can only be faulted for not having more opportunity to use the language. She is learning to read and write in German now and loves the lessons; I believe her firm foundation in the English alphabet has helped here. She has French three times a week and still finds it a great pleasure. She sings beautifully in French and likes to use what she knows in play. When she and the neighbor's child get together, they often pretend they were orphaned in country X and only speak in language X (usually French) and she incorporates whatever she learned that week into her games. Additionally she has Music in school once a week (in German) and once outside (in French) and she is proving to be quite capable in this area. She has ballet on Friday afternoons with a new Israeli teacher who speaks in both French and English during the lessons. All in all, I think I have never seen her happier. She is now six years and nine months old.

Gabriel has advanced so much in English, Spanish, and German. He speaks constantly (too much?) these days. Last night he, Natalie, and my husband came home from watching the new *Star Wars Episode I* movie and he could not stop retelling the plot. He spoke for thirty-five minutes without stopping, and then only because he had to go to the toilet. He tends to begin every sentence with, "Mommy I want to tell you something . . ." and then goes on and on and on. He is using his Spanish in a more active way, though he still prefers to rely on English. When pushed, however, he will use Spanish. Both he and Cristian are enjoying the drive to school in the morning which is conducted solely in Spanish (I'm not there to interfere). At that time Cristian says he speaks more, and his Spanish comprehension is complete. He is thrilled with school, about being one of the "big boys" this year (the three- and four-year-olds are together and since he is four, he is considered "big"). He comes home singing and explaining the day's events in a mixture of languages. I find it very interesting that his vocabulary is completely influenced by repetition and novelty. That is, if he hears a certain word often in Spanish, he only uses the Spanish. If he learned the object's name in German, he uses the German, although in both cases he knows the English equivalent. For example, *"cocodrillo"* and *"dinosaurio"* are always in Spanish (perhaps because I usually don't make that a part of English conversation and my husband does). *"Biene"* is always in German (because they did a big project on bees at school and he checked out a book on it in

German) and *"Haselnuss"* is hazelnut since his class went walking to the park and he brought home a pocket full of them. He is learning quickly and seems very happy. He is now four years and four months old.

Mateo is perhaps the child with the greatest aptitude for foreign languages. He has the clearest pronunciation I ever heard (no "yeah," always "yes"). He is into the copy-cat stage where he imitates everything that Gabriel does, including the things he says. He is attending a French crèche in the mornings, five days a week, and seems to be getting on very well there, though his favorite playmate is a little girl from the neighborhood who speaks English. In any case, the teachers there say he follows directions (when he wants to), and sings in French, or at least makes an effort to do so. I see that he is very comfortable there. He is a true actor, always making faces ("a clown!" he shouts and makes a face, "bad guy!" he shouts and makes another). His vocabulary is very good for his age (funny, not working, apple juice please, popcorn, all done, don't do that, it's mine, what you doing? Why? Mommy cook egg? bath, shower) are a few of the things he has said in the past five minutes. He is trying hard to make sentences and can communicate with non-family members in an adequate way. He is now two years and five months old.

"Faster than a Speeding Bullet" (November 1, 1999)

Mateo is now two-and-a-half years old and each day he seems to scoop up the words around him like a wet cloth to dust. He is repeating everything in a constant chatter, and his growth is especially noticeable in Spanish and French. He answers his father in Spanish usually starting off with a defiant, *"Sí, papi"* or *"No, papi."* He was just yelling about not wanting to get dressed *"No, papi, no pantalón!"* When asked about school he reflects for a moment, unsure how to express his daily affairs in French. But when asked, did Lucy (his teacher) say so-and-so in French?—his face brightens and he says, *"Oui!* Lucy . . ." so-and-so. He is incredible to watch. He knows to speak to Cristian only in Spanish, and me in English. This is a relatively early understanding of this concept. I told him to "say thank you to daddy for the new boots," and he said *"gracias, papi, zapatos."*

Gabriel has reached a point where we feel his German is better than his Spanish. His English is still superior to any other language (in terms of vocabulary and syntax), and his Spanish comprehension is excellent, but he speaks more German than Spanish. This is really a direct consequence of having Spanish only come from one source, his father, whereas he has a day of school, after-school friends, and television in German. He is now conscious of the idea that speaking is vital to the communication process and for survival within the school. He said a new girl joined the school last week but "she couldn't talk," just sing.

Natalie has shown the first signs of losing her child-like innocence. She spends a lot more time dressing in the morning, wondering if she looks like the singers on TV. Her language skills have shown their face again in another way, however, this time in a very unexpected one. She took out a book on sign-language from the library. In the first reading, in the car on the way home, she memorized sixteen of the twenty-six characters. On the second reading she knew twenty, and on the third reading she could show me all twenty-six signs. This is considerably less time than it took her to learn the written English alphabet. Could it be because it was done using her hands as the symbols, not needing the medium of paper and pencil?

A Word About the Diary Notes

These selected diary entries have been shared here to illustrate one family's process through foreign language learning. My three children are a mixed lot. Two I believe have a high aptitude for languages, one does not. The left-handed girl speaks much more than one of the right-handed boys, but not the other. English is close linguistically to German, and Spanish is close to French, perhaps facilitating the children's learning. While they all learned their first two languages in the First Window, two did so in a consistent family strategy, and one did not. All are generally motivated, though I believe this has been more important in the middle child's language acquisition. All have had the very special opportunity of being brought up in a diplomatic family which travels to the countries where their foreign languages are spoken, and therefore they can use them on a daily basis.

These three children, though brought up with the same parents in the same household each have their very own, individualized recipes. For many reasons the children have had varying degrees of success with their languages to date, although I firmly believe all will have fluency levels adequate for schooling in at least three (English, Spanish, and German) of their four languages by the time they complete the Second Window (eight years old), and be able to continue learning even more languages if that is their choice, in the Third Window (from Old Age and Back).

I remain in awe of this entire practice, and the more I learn about how children learn languages, the more impressed I am that my own multilingual children have been so successful.

A FINAL WORD

I sincerely hope that the information within this book serves at least some of the millions of multilingual families around the world who find themselves facing questions we as a family once faced, afloat in a similar linguistic boat on a sea of language choices. I trust that other parents share my appreciation of the amazing way our multilingual children utilize language, which is the most complex achievement of the human brain. I hope this book will lure others to embark on this journey and reap all of the benefits it brings us while raising multilingual children.

——————— *Appendix A* ———————

Finding Language Sources in Scarce Language Environments

- *Language partners*—Arrange for a language exchange with someone at school or in the community. This can be done "consciously" (*i.e.*, "let's find someone to speak Spanish to") or "unconsciously (*i.e.*, "why don't we invite Juan over to play after school tomorrow").
- *Cassettes* of music—Local libraries often have music in various languages, usually in the children's sections, and often with accompanying books.
- *Videos* in foreign language—Often cartoons (Pippi Longstocking, Babar, Madeline, and even classics like Curious George) have been translated into other languages and are available at larger video rental stores.
- *Pen pals overseas*—Initiate a "sister-school" arrangement and write to friends in other countries which speak your desired language.
- *Internet*—Connections with children in other countries is not just an episode from Star Trek, they already exist on a variety of topics (the environment, space, etc.), and hook-ups for spoken (not just typed/written) exchange are now possible. Ask your local computer store for more information, or go onto an Internet search engine like "Yahoo!" to find out more.
- *Bilingual books*—Many children beginning a new language are attracted to "old favorites" in a new language.

Appendix B

The Family Studies: How the Information Was Gathered

The stories included in the *Ingredients* chapter are derived from personal interviews, observations, and informal discussions about multilingualism that I have had the pleasure of participating in as a teacher, student, and mother. Each family was evaluated based on the criteria of 1) the Window of Opportunity in which the languages were learned; 2) the child's aptitude for foreign language based on MLAT criteria; 3) the level of motivation the child had for undertaking the new language; 4) consistency in family language strategy; 5) the amount of opportunity and support the child had when learning his/her languages; 6) the linguistic similarity of the languages being learned; 7) the different abilities of siblings regarding languages; 8) the gender of the child; and 9) the child's hand preference.

The different family combinations here represent just a handful of the types of bilingual families around the world. While limited in number, however, they establish patterns which confirm the importance of key factors in raising multilingual children, as well as illustrating how actual families undertake the challenge of multiple languages in their lives.

The following is a chart of those interviewed for this book. Their methods, strategies, and approaches towards helping their children with foreign language skills are shared here to let readers know that they are not alone in their endeavor, and that there are many paths towards the same goal.

While the sampling here is a good size, it is small in comparison to the possibilities. Given the large number of languages (roughly 6,000) and nationalities (roughly 200), and that bi-, tri-, and quadralinguals are considered here, a much greater number of combinations exist than is presented. Unfortunately not all regions of the world are represented equally in this table. This is due to our travel-pattern as a family and not towards any bias towards particular regions of the world.

On the following chart (Figure B.1) I have listed a sampling of cases which include children from bilingual families, individual students I have had in the past, and adult polyglot friends and relatives.

Hereditary Bilingualism?

A very interesting idea has to do with the hereditary aspect of bilingualism. In the overwhelming majority of cases presented here, children who are multilingual have parents who are also bilingual if not multilingual. This goes back to our story about Berlitz and his language achievements having ancestral roots, which was used to illustrate the Third Window of Opportunity. Could this occur because children imitate the behavior they see in their parents? Because they have the opportunities their "worldly polyglot" parents have? Or because of genetics? Could there actually be a gene for foreign language learning? While this is a fascinating area and many strong feelings have been shared about this topic, scientifically it is still inconclusive (but delicious for speculation!).

All the names have been changed in these cases in order to protect the privacy of the families, though the family facts are true and related as the families themselves have shared them with me.

The Two Most Important Factors

These different family cases indicate the great variety of ways that families can either consciously or unconsciously bring multiple languages into their children's lives. The purpose of this book, however, is to bring to light the factors that make such an endeavor a pleasant and successful one by using these cases to bring to life studies found in the neurological and linguistic experiment rooms.

Which cases had the highest degree of proficiency as measured by the fluency with which the children speak the languages they have been exposed to? Two clear groups emerge: 1) Those who learned the languages simultaneously (early, infant bilinguals) and 2) those who have parents who used consistent language strategies with them. Such cases include Karen (TTTT) who spoke to her children in Swedish while her husband spoke only English; the Chaptal family (M) in which the mother only spoke in Spanish and the father only in French; Case (J) in which the mother spoke in Portuguese and the father in Spanish; Eileen's case (WWWW) in which the mother spoke English and the father German; and Laura (KK) in which the

Figure B.1
Case Studies Chart

Family Code and Community's Dominant Language	Mother's Nationality	Father's Nationality	First Language	Second Language	Third Language	Fourth Language
A French	Colombia	German	English	Spanish	German	French
B French	Nicaragua	American	English	Spanish	French	German
C French	Colombian	Swiss	French	Spanish	German	English
D French	Swiss	Italian	French	German	Italian	
E French	German	German	German	English	French	
F French	Brazilian	Brazilian	English	Portuguese	French	
G French	Colombian	Colombian	Spanish	French	English	
H French	British	Swiss	English	French		
I French	Ecuadorian	Ecuadorian	Spanish	French	English	
J French	Brazilian	Ecuadorian	Portuguese	Spanish	English	French
K French	Ecuadorian	Ecuadorian	Spanish	French	English	
L French	Ecuadorian	Ecuadorian	Spanish	English	French	
M French	Spanish	Swiss	Spanish	French	English	German
N French	USA	USA	English	French		
O German	Czech	Philippine	English	German	Tagalog	Czech
P French	Polish	German	Polish	French	German	
Q French	British	French	English	French		
R French	British	Indian	English	French		
S French	French	Swiss	French	English		
T French	British	Danish	English	Danish	French	
U French	Brazilian	Brazilian	Portuguese	Spanish	French	
V French	American	Norwegian	English	Scandinavia		
W French	Swiss	Swiss	German	French	English	
X French	French	German	French	German		
Y French	Czech	Polish	Czech	German	French	
Z French	Swiss	Swedish	French	Swedish	German	English
AA French	Swiss	Swiss	French	German	English	
BB French	Romanish	Romanian	Romanisch	Hungarian	French	English
CC French	Ecuadorian	Ecuadorian	Spanish	English	French	
DD French	Ecuadorian	Ecuadorian	Spanish	English	French	Italian
EE French	Ecuadorian	Ecuadorian	Spanish	English		
FF Spanish	Ecuadorian	Ecuadorian	Spanish	English	French	
GG French	New Zealand	American	English	French		
HH Spanish	Ecuadorian	Ecuadorian	Spanish	English		
II Spanish	Argentinean	Ecuadorian	Spanish	German	English	
JJ Spanish	Ecuadorian	Swedish	Spanish	German	English	Swedish
KK Spanish	Hungarian	Ecuadorian	Spanish	Hungarian		
LL Spanish	British	Ecuadorian	Spanish	English		
MM Spanish	Ecuadorian	Ecuadorian	Spanish	English		
NN Spanish	Ecuadorian	Ecuadorian	Spanish	English	French	
OO Spanish	German	Ecuadorian	Spanish	German	English	
PP Spanish	German	Ecuadorian	Spanish	German	English	
QQ Spanish	Nicaragua	Italian	Spanish	Italian	English	
RR Spanish	American	Ecuadorian	Spanish	English		
SS Hebrew	American	Israeli	English	Hebrew	German	Spanish
TT Hebrew	Israeli	Israeli	Hebrew	English		
UU Tagalog	Philippine	Philippine	Tagalog	English	Spanish	
VV German	Austrian	Austrian	German	English		

Figure B.1 (continued)

	Mother's Nationality	Father's Nationality	First Language	Second Language	Third Language	Fourth Language
WW English	Chinese	American	English	Chinese		
XX German	German	German	German	English		
YY English	American	American	English	Hebrew		
ZZ Spanish	Argentinean	Argentinean	Spanish	English		
AAA Spanish	Argentinean	Argentinean	Spanish	English		
BBB Spanish	German	French	Spanish	French	German	English
CCC Japanese	Japanese	French	Japanese	French	English	
DDD English	Chinese	Japanese	Japanese	English	Chinese	
EEE English	Ecuadorian	Ecuadorian	English	Spanish		
FFF English	Ecuadorian	Italian	English	Spanish	Italian	
GGG English	American	American	English	Spanish		
HHH Spanish	Ecuadorian	Ecuadorian	Spanish	English	French	
III Spanish	German	French	German	Spanish	French	English
JJJ Japanese	Japanese	American	Japanese	English		
KKK Korean	Korean	Korean	Korean	Japanese	English	
LLL Korean	Korean	Korean	Korean	English	Japanese	
MMM Spanish	Ecuadorian	Hungarian	Spanish	English	French	
NNN Spanish	Ecuadorian	Hungarian	Spanish	English	German	
OOO Arabic	Lebanese	Lebanese	Arabic	French	English	
PPP Spanish	Lebanese	Lebanese	French	Arabic	English	Spanish
RRR German	Swiss	Swiss	German	French	English	
SSS German	German	German	German	English	French	
TTT Greek	Cyprus	Cyprus	Greek	English		

Friend Current Language Community	Mother's Nationality	Father's Nationality	First Language	Second Language	Third Language	Fourth Language
AAAA Spanish	Ecuadorian	Ecuadorian	Spanish	German	English	
BBBB French	American	Ecuadorian	English	Spanish	German	French
CCCC French	Greek	Greek	Greek	English	Spanish	French
DDDD German	Ecuadorian	German	Spanish	German	English	
EEEE English	American	American	English	German		
FFFF English	Chinese	Chinese	Cantonese	English	Spanish	U.S. Sign
GGGG Spanish	Ecuadorian	Ecuadorian	Spanish	English	French	
HHHH Spanish	Ecuadorian	Ecuadorian	Spanish	German	English	French
IIII Spanish	Ecuadorian	Ecuadorian	Spanish	English		

Relative	Mother's Nationality	Father's Nationality	First Language	Second Language	Third Language	Fourth Language
JJJJ English	American	American	English	Spanish		
LLLL Spanish	Ecuadorian	Ecuadorian	Spanish	German	English	
MMMM Spanish	Ecuadorian	Ecuadorian	Spanish	German	English	
NNNN Spanish	Ecuadorian	Ecuadorian	Spanish	German	English	
OOOO English	Japanese	Japanese	Japanese	English	Okinawan	
PPPP English	American	American	English	Japanese		
QQQQ English	American	American	English	Japanese		
RRRR Spanish	Ecuadorian	Ecuadorian	Spanish	English		
SSSS French	Brazilian	Swiss	French	Portuguese	English	German
TTTT French	Swedish	Swiss	French	Swedish	English	
UUUU French	Nicaraguan	Nicaraguan	English	Spanish	French	German
VVVV French	Spanish	Spanish	German	Spanish		
WWWW French	Irish	German	English	German	French	

mother spoke Hungarian and the father Spanish. *In other words, whether it was the "simple" case of a bilingual, or the "complex" situation of a quadralingual, the degree of success was more correlated to when the language was introduced and how the parents exposed the children to it, than to the number of languages they incorporated.* There are no unsuccessful bilinguals who were simultaneous bilinguals (learned their languages from birth) if their parents were consistent in strategy. All children who learned two or more languages from birth were fluent bilinguals. Equally important but twice as distressing, however, were the cases of children who bordered on "semilingualism" who were not fluent in any of their languages. Such cases include the Brazilian-Swiss couple (Case SSSS) whose sons received a mixture of Portuguese, German, French, and English while growing up; the case of the Kurtz family (C) which mixed German, French, Spanish, and English with their children, or case (A) in which the parents often did not speak their native languages to their children and often mixed German, Spanish, English, and French when speaking to each other. These cases were not as successful as the others for the obvious reason that the children were far beyond the normal limits of separating their languages and in developing meta-language skills for thinking. What caused this language development delay? In most cases it could be blamed on the inconsistent mix of languages that their parents dished out to them. Happily, this too could be resolved, however. There generally seems to be a cure for the dreaded semilingualism disease by the time children reach school and find a haven of consistency within the walls of the classroom. Once offered linguistic consistency, the children were able to correctly categorize language input into pockets of "French" or "English" or "German" and to begin associating individuals with different languages. They then move on to organizing their own thinking skills and move on to deeper thinking skills because their toolbox wasn't a jumble anymore.

In a word then, or rather three, the key seems to be in Timing, Strategy, and Consistency. The most important factors influencing the levels of success in these cases were the Windows of Opportunity and the Timing of language introduction, the Strategies used to teach the second language to the children, and the Consistency with which the languages were maintained in the children's lives.

Glossary

Affect—Something that impresses your mind or moves your feelings.

Amygdala—Part of the limbic system next to the temporal lobe in the brain, involved with emotions.

Angular gyrus—The part of the brain which associates the visual form of a word with its corresponding sound.

Aphasia—The loss of a previously held ability to speak or understand spoken or written language, due to disease or injury of the brain.

Arcuate fasciculus—A bundle of fibers in the brain connecting Broca's area and Wernicke's area (two areas involved with speech).

Auditory cortex—The part of the brain which receives the spoken word.

Bilingual—Involving or using two languages.

Broca's area—The speech area of the brain which "tells" the mouth how a word should be pronounced.

Cerebral dominance—Which hemisphere (right or left) of the brain is "stronger"; most people are left-hemisphere dominant for languages, for example.

Cognitive/Cognition—Having to do with thought or thinking. The act or process of knowing; perception.

Effect—A result or consequence.

ESL—English as a Second Language.

ESL track—The school program catering to non-native English-language speakers. The people in this group are sometimes referred to as "language minority learners."

Frontal lobes—The part of the brain related to logical thinking, located just behind the forehead.

Glottal stop—A consonant sound which forms in the glottis (in the throat), as in the Scottish pronunciation of the *t*-sound of *little* or *bottle*.

Left hemisphere—The left half of the brain.

Linguistic relationship between languages—The historical connection between different languages identifying their similarities and differences.

Linguistics—The science and study of language.

Monolingual—One language.

Motor cortex—The part of the brain (related to speech) which drives the muscles of the lips, the tongue, the larynx, etc., and the hand (related to writing).

Multilingual—Involving or using many languages.

Multiliteracy skills—The ability to read and write in more than one language.

Multiliterate—The ability to read and/or write in several languages.

Myelin insulation in the brain—The connections between synapses in the brain which speed up impulses and make information easier to retrieve.

Neocortex—The newest part of the brain in evolution which is related to higher level thinking processes, such as language and reasoning.

Neurobiology—The science studying the connection between biology and the physiology of the nervous system (including the brain).

Neurolinguistics—The study of the neurological processes underlying the development and use of language.

Neurology—The science of the nerves and nervous system, including those found in the brain.

Neuron—A specialized, impulse-connecting cell that is the functional unit of the nervous system; a cell in the brain.

Neuropsychology—The branch of medicine related to the physical foundations of mental functions and problems.

Orthography—Writing. The art of writing words with the proper letters, according to accepted usage and correct spelling.

Polyglot—Someone who speaks and/or writes two or more languages. Multilingual.

Right hemisphere—The right side of the brain.

Semilingual—A person who has partial or incomplete working knowledge of a language or languages. Someone without reflective meta-language skills in any language.

Synapse—The electrical connection between neurons in the brain.

Synesthesia—A sensation produced in one modality when a stimulus is applied to another modality, as when the hearing of a certain sound induces the visualization of a certain color.

Syntax—The grammatical rules of a language.

Visual cortex—The area of the brain concerned with stimuli that is seen.

Wernicke's area—The area of the brain concerned with speech and where the auditory pattern of words is deciphered.

Window of Opportunity—The special times when certain skills or intelligences can be learned in a human's lifetime with the best results.

Bibliography

Adams, Marilyn Jager. *Beginning to Read, Thinking and Learning About Print*. Cambridge, MA: The MIT Press, A Bradford Book, Ninth Printing, 1996.

Aimard, Paule. *L'Enfant et la Magie du Language*. Paris: Editions Robert Laffont, 1984.

Albert, M. L. and L. Obler. *The Bilingual Brain: Neuropsychological and Neurolinguistic Aspects of Bilingualism*. New York: Academia Press, 1979.

Allemann-Ghionda, Cristina. *Multiculture et Education en Europe*. Bern, Switzerland: Peter Lang Publisher, 1997.

Allemann-Ghionda, Cristina, Claire de Goumoëns, and Christiane Perregaux. *Pluralité et culturelle dans la formation des enseignant*. Programme National de Recherche 33. Bern, Switzerland: Universitaires Fribourg, Suisse, 1999.

Andersson, T. *A Guide to Family Reading in Two Languages, The Preschool Years*. Virginia: National Clearinghouse for Bilingual Education, 1981.

Arnberg, Lenore. *Raising Children Bilingually: The Pre-School Years*. England: Multilingual Matters Ltd., 1987.

Atkinson, Martin. *Explanations in the Study of Child Language Development*. Gen. ed. W. Siney Allen, B. Comrie, C. J. Fillmore, E. J. A. Henderson, F. W. Householder, R. Lass, J. Lyons, R. B. Le Page, P. H.

Matthews, F. R. Palmer, R. Posner, J. L. M. Trim. Cambridge, England: Cambridge Studies in Linguistics, Cambridge University Press 1982.

August, Diane and Kenji Hakuta, eds. *Educating Language Minority Children*. New York: National Academy Press, 1998.

Baker, Colin. *A Parents and Teachers Guide to Bilingualism*, 2nd edition. England: Multilingual Matters, Ltd., 2000.

Beardsmore, Hugo Baetens, ed. *Elements of Bilingual Theory*. Brussels: Tidscrift van de Vrije Universiteit, 1981.

Beardsmore, Hugo, Baetens, ed. *European Models of Bilingual Education*. England: Multilingual Matters, Ltd., 1993.

Begley, Sharon. "Your Child's Brain." *Newsweek Magazine* (19 February 1996).

Begley, Sharon. "How to Build Your Baby's Brain." *Newsweek Magazine* (Spring/Summer 1997): 28–32.

Belcher, Diane, and George Briane, eds. *Academic Writing in a Second Language, Essays on Research and Pedagogy*. New Jersey: Ablex Publishing Corp, 1995.

Bialystok, Ellen, ed. *Language Processing in Bilingual Children*. Cambridge, England: Cambridge University Press, 1991.

Bialystok, Ellen, ed., and Kenji Hakuta, contr. *In Other Words: The Science and Psychology of Second Language Acquisition*. New York: Basic Books, 1995.

Blakeslee, Sandra. "Making Baby Smart: Words Are the Way In Year One, Hearing Talk Shapes Mind." *International Herald Tribune* 18 April 1997. New York Times Service, 1997.

Bloomfield, L. *Language*. New York: Holt, Rinehart and Winston, 1933.

Calfee, Robert C. "Assessment of Independent Reading Skills: Basic Research and Practical Applications." In A. S. Reber and D. L. Scarborough, *Toward a Psychology of Reading* 289–323. Hillsdale, NJ: Lawrence Erlbaum Associates, 1977.

Calfee, Robert C., Betty J. Mace-Matluck and A. Hoover Wesley. *Teaching Reading to Bilingual Children Study, Vols. I, 6*. Document BRS-84-R. 1-I, 6. Preston C. Kronkosky, Executive Director. Texas: Southwest Educational Developmental Laboratory, November, 1984.

Calfee, R. C., and P. Drum. "Research on Teaching Reading." In *Handbook of Research on Teaching*. Ed. M. C. Wittrock. 804–849. New York: Macmillan, 1986.

Carrell, Patricia L., Joanne Levine, and Daniel Eskey, eds. *Interactive Approaches to Second Language Reading*. Cambridge, England: The Cambridge Applied Linguistics Theory, Cambridge University Press, 1989.

Carroll, J. B. "Psychological and Educational Research into Second Language

Teaching to Young Children." In *Languages and the Young School Child*. H. H. Stern. London: Oxford University Press, 1969.

Carroll, J. B., and S. M. Sapon. *Modern Language Apitude Test*. New York: The Psychological Corporation, 1958.

Chaudron, Craig. *Second Language Classrooms, Research on Teaching and Learning*. Cambridge, England: The Cambridge Applied Linguistic Theory, Cambridge University Press, 1988.

Ching, Doris C. *Reading and the Bilingual Child*. A reading aids series, California State University at Los Angeles. Newark and Delaware: International Reading Association, 1976.

Chomsky, Noam. *Reflections of Language*. New York: Pantheon Books, 1975.

Cole, S. and S. Scribner. Introduction to *Mind in Society*. Eds. L. S. Vygotsky, M. Cole, V. John-Steiner, S. Scribner and E. Souberman. Cambridge, MA: Harvard University Press, 1978.

Coltheart, M. *When Can Children Learn to Read—And What Should They Be Taught?* In T. G. Waller and G. E. Mackinnon (eds.), *Reading Research: Advances in Theory and Practice*, Vol. I. New York: Academic Press, 1979.

Coltheart, M., K. Patterson, and J. Marshall, eds. *Deep Dyslexia*. London: Routledge & Kegan Paul, 1980.

Comrie, Bernard, ed. *The World's Languages*. London: Routledge, 1989.

Cowley, Geoffrey. "The Language Explosion." *Newsweek Magazine* Special Ed. (Spring/Summer 1997): 17.

Cumming, Alister, H., ed. *Bilingual Performance in Reading and Writing*. Amsterdam: John Benjamin's Publishing Company, 1994.

Cummins, Jim. "The cognitive development of children in immersion programs." *Canadian Modern Language Review*, 34 (1978): 855–883.

Cummins, Jim. "The Construct of Language Proficiency in Bilingual Education." In the *Georgetown Round Table on Languages and Linguistics*. Washington, DC: March 1980.

Cummins, Jim. "Interdependence of first and second language proficiency in bilingual children." In *Language Processing in Bilingual Children*. Ed. E. Bialystok. Cambridge, England: Cambridge University Press, 1991.

Curtain, H. and C. Pesola. *Languages and Children: Making the Match*. 2d ed. White Plains, NY: Longman, 1994.

Dale, Philip, and David Ingram, eds. "Child Language—An International Perspective" Selected Papers from the First International Congress for the Study of Child Language. Baltimore, MD: University Park Press, 1981.

Dechert, Hans W., ed. *Current Trends in European Second Language Acquisition Research*. England: Multilingual Matters, Ltd., 1990.

Dechert, Hans W. and Manfred Raupauch, eds. *Interlingual Processe*. Tubinge: Gunter Van Verlag, 1989.

Dorman, Glen. *How to Teach Your Baby to Read*. London: Pan Books, 1975.

Dörnyei, Z. "Ten commandments for motivating language learners." Paper presented at TESOL, Chicago, March 1996.

Dunn, Opal. *Help Your Child With a Foreign Language, A Parent's Handbook*. London: Headway, Hodder & Stoughton, 1994.

Edelsky, Carole. *Writing in a Bilingual Program-Había Una Vez*. Arizona State University. New Jersey: Ablex Publishing Corporation, 1986.

Elliot, Alison J. *Child Language*. Cambridge: Cambridge University Press, 1988.

Ellis, Andrew W. *Reading, Writing and Dyslexia, A Cognitive Analysis*. 2d ed. New Jersey: Lawrence Erlbaum Associates, 1994.

Erickson, Joan Good and Donald R. Omark, eds. *Communication Assessment of the Bilingual Bicultural Child, Issues and Guidelines*. Baltimore, MD: University Park Press, 1981.

Ersenson, Jon. *Aphasia in Children*. New York: Harper and Row, 1972.

Flurkey, Alan D., and Richard J. Meyer, eds. *Under the Whole Language Umbrella, Many Cultures, Many Voices*. Illinois: National Council of Teachers of English, 1995.

Galloway, Linda. "Language impairment and recovery in polyglot aphasia: a case of a heptaglot." In *Aspects of Bilingualism*. Ed. M. Paradis. Columbia: Hornbeam Press, 1978.

Gardner, Howard. *The Shattered Mind*. New York: Basic Books, 1975.

Gardner, Howard. *Art, Mind and Brain, A Cognitive Approach to Creativity*. New York: Basic Books, 1982.

Gardner, Howard. *Frames of Mind*. New York: Basic Books 1983.

Gardner, Howard. *Multiple Intelligences, the Theory in Practice*. New York: Basic Books 1993.

Gass, Susan and Jacquelyn Schachter. *Linguistic Perspectives on Second Language Acquisition*. Cambridge, England: The Cambridge Applied Linguistic Theory, Cambridge University Press, 1988.

Gass, Susan, Carolyn Madden, Dennis Preston, and Larry Selinker, eds. *Variation in Second Language Acquisition*, Vol. 1 *Discoveries and Pragmatics*, and Vol. II *Psycholinguistic Issues*. England: Multilingual Matters, Ltd., 1989.

Genesee, Fred. "Is there an optimal age for starting second language learning?" *Journal of Education* 13 (1978): 145–154.

Genesee, Fred, W. E. Lambert, L. Mononen, M. Seitz, and R. Starch. "Language Processing in Bilinguals." *Brain and Language* 5 (1979): 1–12.

Geschwind, N. "Why Orton was right." *Annals of Dyslexia* 32 (1982): 13–30.

Geschwind, Norman. "Specializations of the Human Brain." From reading packet for Neuropsychology course by Professor Mark Greenberg. Massachusetts: Book Tech, 1997.

Gleitman, Lila R., and Mark Liberman, eds. *An Invitation to Cognitive Science: Language, Volume 1*. 2d ed. Ed. Daniel N. Osherson. Cambridge, MA: Bradford Books, The MIT Press, 1995.

Gleitman, Lila R. and Elissa L. Newport. "The Invention of Language by Children: Environmental and Biological Influences on the Acquisition of Language." In *An Invitation to Cognitive Science, Second Edition, Volume 1*. Ed. Gleitman and Liberman. Cambridge, MA: The MIT Press, 1995.

Goodman, Kenneth, Yetta Goodman, and Barbara Flores. *Reading in the Bilingual Classroom: Literacy and Biliteracy*. Virginia: National Clearing House for Bilingual Education, 1984.

Gorman, Christine. "How Gender Can Bend Your Thinking." *Time Magazine* (31 July 1995): 41.

Greenberg, Mark S. "Neuropsychology." Harvard University Extension course. Spring 1997. Use of: *Human Neuropsychology*, 4th Ed.

Grosjean, François. *Life With Two Languages, An Introduction to Bilingualism*. Cambridge, MA: Harvard University Press, 1982.

Grunwell, Pamela, ed. *Developmental Speech Disorders, Clinical Issues and Practical Implications*. London: Whurr Publishers, Ltd., 1995.

Hagège, Claude. *L'Enfant Aux Deux Langues*. Paris: Edition Odile Jacob, 1996.

Hakuta, Kenji. *Mirror of Language, The Debate on Bilingualism*. New York: Basic Books, 1986.

Harding, Edith and Philip Riley. *The Bilingual Family, A Handbook for Parents*. Ninth Printing. Cambridge, England: Cambridge University Press, 1996.

Harley, Birgit. *Age in Second Language Acquisition*. England: Multilingual Matters, Ltd., 1986.

Harley, Birgit, Patrick Allen, Jim Cummins, and Merrill Swain, eds. *The Development of Second Language Proficiency*. Cambridge Applied Linguistics Series. Eds. Michael H. Long and Jack C. Richards. Cambridge, England: Cambridge University Press, 1990.

Harris, Judith Rich. *The Nurture Assumption*. New York: The Free Press, 1998.

Hatch, E., ed. *Second Language Acquisition: A Book of Readings*. Massachusetts: Newbury House, 1978.

Haugen, R. "Bilingualism as a social and personal problem." In *Active Methods and Modern Aids in the Teaching of Foreign Languages*. Ed. R. Filipovic, 1–14. London, England: Oxford University Press, 1972.

Haugenm, E. *The Norwegian Language in America: A Study of Bilingual Behavior*. 2d rev. ed. Bloomington: Indiana University Press, 1969.

Homel, Peter, Michael Palij, and Doris Aaronson. *Childhood Bilingualism: Aspects of Linguistic Cognition, and Social Development*. New Jersey: Lawrence Erlbaum Associates, 1987.

Hudelson, Sarah, ed. *Learning to Read in Different Languages, Linguistics and Literacy Series: 1*. Ed. Roger W. Shuy. Washington DC: Center For Applied Linguistics, 1981.

Hughes, Felicity. *Reading and Writing Before School.* London: Cape Press, 1971.

Jacobs, W. J., and L. Nadel. *"Stress-induced recovery of fears and phobias,"* Psychological Review, 92 (1985): 512–531.

Johnson, Wendell. *Stuttering in children and adults: Thirty years of research at the University of Iowa.* Assisted by Ralph Leutenegger. Minneapolis: University of Minnesota Press, 1967.

Kessler, Carolyn. *The Acquisition of Syntax in Bilingual Children.* Georgetown University School of Languages and Linguistics. Washington, DC: Georgetown University Press, 1971.

Kielhöfer, B., and S. Jonekeit. *Zweisprachige Erziehung.* Tübingen: Stauffenberg–Verlag, 1983.

Kim, K. and J. Hirsch. "Distinct Cortical areas associated with native and second languages." *Nature* 388 (July 10, 1997): 1716.

Klein, Wolfgang. *Second Language Acquisition.* Cambridge, England: Cambridge University Press, 1986.

Krashen, Stephen D. *Principles and Practices in Second Language Acquisition.* California: Alemany Press, 1982.

Krashen, Stephen D. *The Natural Approach to Language Acquisition in the Classroom.* New York: Prentice Hall, 1996.

Krashen, Stephen D. *Foreign Language Education the Easy Way.* California: Language Education Association, 1998.

Krasnegor, Norman A., Duane M. Rumbaugh, Richard Schiefelbuch, and Michael Studdert-Kennedy, eds. *Biological and Behavioral Determinants of Language Development.* New Jersey: Lawrence Erlbaum Associates, 1991.

Kuhl, P. K., K. A. Williams, F. Lacerda, K. N. Stevens, and B. Lindblom. "Linguistic experience alters phonetic perception in infants by 6 months of age." *Science* 255 (1992): 606–608.

Laffey, James L., and Roger Shuy, eds. *Language Differences: Do they interfere?* Newark and Delaware: International Reading Association, 1973.

Lamb, Sydney M. *Pathways of the Brain: The neurocognitive basis of language.* Amsterdam: John Benjamins, Publisher, 1999.

Lave, Jean and Etienne Wenger. *Situated Learning, Legitimate Peripheral Participation.* Cambridge, England: Cambridge University Press, 1996.

Law, James, ed. *The Early Identification of Language Impairment in Children.* London: Chapman & Hall, 1992.

Lees, Janet and Shelagh Urwin. *Children With Language Disorders.* London: Whurr Publishers, 1996.

Lennenberg, Eric H. *Biological Foundations of Language.* New York: John Wiley and Son, 1967.

Leopold, Werner. *Speech Development of a Bilingual Child, A Linguist's Record,* vol. 1 *Vocabulary Growth in the First Two Years;* Vol. II *Sound-Learning in the First Two Years*; Vol. III *Grammar and General Problems in the First Two Years*; Vol. IV *Diary From Age Two*. New York: AMS Press, 1939–1949.

Luelsdorff, Philip, A. *Developmental Orthography*. Amsterdam: John Benjamins Publisher, 1991.

Luria, A. R. and F. Yudovich. *Speech and the Development of Mental Processes in the Child*. Ed. Joan Simo. London: Staples Press, 1959.

Lvovich, Natasha. *The Multilingual Self, An Inquiry into Language Learning*. New Jersey: Lawrence Erlbaum, Associates, 1997.

Mackey, William F., and Theodore Andersson, eds. *Bilingualism in Early Childhood*. Studies in Bilingual Education Series. Massachusetts: Newbury House, 1977.

Mai, Jurgen K., Joseph K. Assheuer, and George Paxinos. *Atlas of the Human Brain*. New York: Academic Press, 1998.

McLaughlin, Barry. *Second-Language Acquisition in Childhood, Vol. 1: Preschool Children*. 2d ed. New Jersey: Lawrence Erlbaum Associates, 1985a.

McLaughlin, Barry. *Second-Language Acquisition in Childhood, Vol. 2: School Age Children*. New Jersey: Lawrence Erlbaum Associates, 1985b.

McLaughlin, Barry. *Theories of Second-Language Learning*. New York: Edward Arnold Publishers, 1987.

McLaughlin, Barry. "The relationship between first and second languages: language proficiency and language aptitudes." Chap. 12 in *The Development of Second Language Proficiency*. Ed. Harley, Cummins, and Allen 167. Cambridge, England: Cambridge University Press, 1990.

McLaughlin, B. and R. Nation. "Experts and novices: An information-processing approach to the 'good language learner' problem." *Applied psycholinguistics* 7 (1986): 41–56.

Morehead, Donald M., and Ann Morehead. *Normal and Deficient Child Language*. Baltimore, MD: University Park Press, 1976.

Obler, Loraine and K. Hyltenstam, eds. *Bilingualism Across the Life Span. Aspects of Acquisition, Maturity and Loss*. Cambridge, England: Cambridge University Press, 1989.

Obler, Loraine and Lise Menn, eds. *Perception, Language and Linguistics*. New York: Academic Press, Inc., 1982a.

Obler, Loraine and Lise Menn, eds. "Exceptional Language and Linguistics." Chap. 19 in *The Parsimonious Bilingual*. New York: Academic Press, 1982b.

Ojemann, G. A. and H. A. Whitaker. "The bilingual brain." *Archives of Neurology* 35 (1978): 409–412.

O'Maggio-Hadley, A. C. *Teaching Language in Context*. Boston: Heinle & Heinle, 1993.

Omark, Donald R., and Joan Good Erickson, eds. *The Bilingual Exceptional Child*. San Diego: College Hill Press, 1983.

Ornstein, Robert and Richard F. Thompson. *The Amazing Brain*. Boston: Houghton Mifflin Company, 1986.

Osborn, Terry. *Critical Reflection and the Foreign Language Classroom*. Connecticut: Bergin & Garvey, 2000.

Osherson, Daniel N., ed. "An Invitation to Cognitive Science," Vol. 1 Language. 2d ed. Eds. Lila R. Gleitman and Mark Liberman. Cambridge, MA: The MIT Press, 1997.

Paradis, Michel. "Bilingualism and Aphasia." In *Studies in Neurolinguistics*. Vol. 3. Eds. H. A. Whitaker and H. Whitaker. New York: Academia Press, 1977.

Paradis, Michel. *Aspects of Bilingualism*. Columbia: Hornbeam Press, 1978.

Paradis, Michel, ed. *Readings on Aphasia in Bilinguals and Polyglots*. Canada: Didier, 1983.

Paradis, Michel. "On representation of two languages in one brain." *Language Sciences* 7 (1985): 1–40.

Paradis, Michel. "Bilingualism and polyglot aphasia." In *Handbook of Neuropsychology*. Vol. 2. Ed. Boller, F. and Grafman, J. Amsterdam: John Benjamin's Publishers, 1989.

Paradis, Michel. *Aspects of Bilingual Aphasia*. New York: Pergamon Press, 1995.

Paradis, Michel, Hiroko Hagiwara, and Nancy Hidebrandt. *Neurolinguistic Mapping of the Japanese Writing System*. New York: Academic Press, 1985.

Peal, Elizabeth and Wallace Lambert. "The relationship of bilingualism to intelligence." *Psychological Monographs*. 76, no. 27 (1962): 1–23.

Penfield, W. and L. Roberts. *Speech and Brain Mechanisms*. Princeton, New Jersey: Princeton University Press, 1959.

Perry, Bruce. Quoted in "How to Build Your Baby's Brain," by Sharon Begley. *Newsweek Magazine* (Spring/Summer 1997): 31–32.

Pinker, Steven. *The Language Instinct, How the Mind Creates Language*. New York: William Morrow and Company, 1994.

Pinker, Steven. "Language Acquisition." In Gleitman and Liberman, eds. *An Invitation to Cognitive Science*, Vol. 1, 2d ed. Ed. Daniel N. Osheron, Cambridge, MA: Bradford Books, The MIT Press, 1995.

Pollock, David. *Third Culture Kids Syndrome*. Washington, DC: Foreign Service Youth Foundation, 1991.

Pollock, David and Ruth E. Van Reken. *The Third Culture Kid Experience: Growing Up Among Worlds*. Maine: Intercultural Press, 1999.

Restak, Richard. *The Brain*. New York: Bantam Books, 1984.

Ricciardelli, Lina A. "Creativity and Bilingualism." *Journal of Creative Behaviour* 26, no. 4 (1992): 242–254.

Richards, J. C. and T. S. Rodgers. *Approaches and methods in language teaching: A description and analysis*. Cambridge, England: Cambridge University Press, 1986.

Rogoff, Barbara. *Apprenticeship in Thinking, Cognitive Development in Social Context*. New York and Oxford, England: Oxford University Press, 1990.

Ronjat, Jules. *Le development du langage observe chez un enfant bilingüe*. Paris: Librarie Ancienne H. Champion, 1913.

Rosier, P., and M. Farella. "Bilingual Education at Rock Point, Some Early Results." *TESOL Quarterly* 10, no 4 (1976): 379–388.

Rutherford, William, ed. *Language Universals and Second Language Acquisition*. Amsterdam: John Benjamin's Publishers, 1984.

Saer, D. J. "The effects of bilingualism on intelligence." *British Journal of Psychology* 14 (1923): 25–38.

Sasanuma, Sumiko. "Kana and Kanji Processing in Japanese Aphasics." *Brain and Language* 2 (1975): 369–383.

Saunders, George. *Bilingual Children: Guidance for the Family*. England: Multilingual Matters, Ltd., 1982.

Saunders, George. *Bilingual Children: from Birth to Teens*. England: Multilingual Matters, Ltd., 1982.

Saville, M., and R. Troike. "Handbook of Bilingual Education." *TESOL Quarterly* (1971).

Schaschter, Jacquelyn and Susan Gass, eds. *Second Language Classroom Research, Issues and Opportunities*. New Jersey: Lawrence Erlbaum Associates, Publishers, 1996.

Schumann, John H. *The Neurobiology of Affect in Language*. Michigan: Blackwell Publisher, Language Learning Research Club, University of Michigan, 1997.

Shrum, Judith L. and Eileen W. Glisan. *Teacher's Handbook: Contextualized language instruction*. 2d ed. Boston: Heinle & Heinle, 1999.

Sierra Martínez, Fermin. *La ensenanza de segundas lenguas y/o lenguas extranjeras*. Número 14. Netherlands: Editorial Rodopi, 1994.

Sierra Martínez, Fermin, Merce Pujol Berche, and Harm den Boer, eds. *Las lenguas en la Europa Comunitaria, La adquisición de segundas lenguas y/o de lenguas extranjeras*. Número 13. Netherlands: Editoral Rodopi, 1994.

Simoes, Antonios, Jr., ed. *The Bilingual Child, Research and Analysis of Existing Educational Themes*. New York: Academia Press, 1976.

Skehan, Peter. *A Cognitive Approach to Language Learning*. England: Oxford University Press, 1998.

Skutnabb-Kangas, Tove. *Teaching Migrant Children's Mother Tongue and Learning the Language of the Host Country in the Context of the Socio-cultural situation of the Migrant Family*. Tampere, Finland: Tutkimuk-sia Research Reports, 1976.

Skutnabb-Kangas, Tove. *Multilingualism for all (European Studies on Multilingualism)*. Germany: Swets & Zeitlinger, 1995.

Skutnabb-Kangas, Tove and Robert Phillipson, eds. *Linguistic Human Rights, Overcoming Linguistic Discrimination*. Berlin: Mouton de Gruyter Publishers, 1994.

Slobin, Dan Isaac, ed. *The Crosslinguistic Study of Language Acquisition*, Vols. 1 *The Data* and 2 *Theoretical Issues* (1985), Vol. 3. New Jersey: Lawrence Erlbaum, 1992.

Smiley, Lydia R. and Peggy A. Goldstein. *Language Delays and Disorders: From Research to Practice*. San Diego, CA: Singular Group Publishing, 1998.

Snow, Catherine E., and M. Hoefnagel-Höhle. "Age differences in second language acquisition." In *Second Language Acquisition, A Book of Readings*. Ed. E. Hatch. Massachusetts: Newbury House, Rowley, 1978.

Snow, Catherine and Charles Ferguson, eds. *Talking to Children*. Cambridge, England: Cambridge University Press, 1979.

Snow, Catherine and A. Ninio. "The contracts of literacy: What children learn from learning to read books." In *Emergent literacy: Writing and reading*. Ed. W. H. Teale and E. Salzby. 116–138. Norwood, NJ: Ablex Publishing Corporation, 1986.

Springer, Sally P., and Georg Deutsch. *Left Brain, Right Brain: Perspective from Cognitive Neuroscience*. New York: Worth Publications, 1997.

Stevens, Florence E. *Strategies in Second Language Acquisition*. Quebec, Canada: Eden Press, 1984.

Street, Brian, ed. *Cross-cultural Approaches to Literacy*. Cambridge Studies of Oral and Literate Cultures. Cambridge, England: Cambridge University Press, 1993.

Swain, M. "Time and timing in bilingual education." *Language and Learning* 31 (1981): 1–15.

Taeschner, Traute. *The Sun Is Feminine: A Study on Language Acquisition in Bilingual Children*. Berlin: Spring-Verlag, 1983.

"Teaching Children to Read: Politics Colors Debate Over Methods." *The New York Times* 11 May 1997.

Titone, R. *A Guide to Bilingual Reading*. Rome: Armando Press, 1977a.

Titone, R. *Le Bilinguisme Précoce*. Trans. Gustavo Soto. Brussels: Charles Dessert Editeur, 1977b.

Tremblay, P. F. and R. C. Garner. "Expanding the motivation construct in language learning." *The Modern Language Journal* 79 (1995): 505–520.

Tsushima, T., O. Takizawa, M. Sasaki, S. Shiraki, K. Nishi, M. Kohno, P. Menyuk, and C. Best. *Discrimination of English/r-l/and/w-y/by Japanese infants 6–12 months. Language-specific developmental changes in speech perception abilities*. Paper presented at the International Conference on Spoken Language. Yokohama, Japan: 1994.

Verhoeven, Ludo. *Functional Literacy, Theoretical Issues and Educational Implications*. Amsterdam: John Benjamin's Publishers, 1994.

Vihmen, Marilyn May. "Formulas in First and Second Language Acquisition." Chap. 16 in *Perception, Language and Linguistics*. Ed. L. Obler and L. Menn. New York: Academic Press, 1982.

Vygotsky, L. S. *Pensée et langue*. Paris: Messidor/Editions Sociales, 1985.

Wagner, Daniel, ed. *The Future of Literacy in a Changing World*. Comparative and International Education Series, Vol. 1. Oxford, England: Pergamon Press, 1987.

Werker, J. F. and R. C. Tees. "Cross-language speech perception: Evidence for perceptual reorganization during the first year of life." *Infant Behaviour and Development* 7 (1984a): 49–63.

Werker, Janet F. "Exploring Developmental Changes in Cross-Language Speech Perception." Chap. 4 in *An Invitation to Cognitive Science, Vol. 1, Language*, 2d ed. Gen. Ed. Daniel N. Osherson. Vol. Ed. Lila R. Gleitman and Mark Liberman. Cambridge, MA: The MIT Press, 1997.

Werner, H. and B. Kaplan. *Symbol formation*. New York: John Wiley and Sons, 1963.

Whitaker H. A., D. Bub, and S. Leventer. "Neurolinguistic aspects of language acquisition and bilingualism." In *Native language and foreign language acquisition*. Ed. H. Winitz. New York: The New York Academy of Sciences, 1981.

Willis, Thomas. *Cerebri Anatome (Anatomy of the Brain)*. Illustrated by Sir Christopher Wren. England: Publisher unknown, 1664.

Winitz, H., ed. *Native language and foreign language acquisition*. New York: The New York Academy of Sciences, 1981.

Young, Mark C. *Guinness Book of World Records 1999*. New York: Bantam Books, 1999.

Index

About the Author

TRACY TOKUHAMA-ESPINOSA is a native of California who studied for her Master's of Education at Harvard University, and has taught in international schools in Japan, Ecuador, and France. Tracey has given numerous workshops on raising multilingual children to schools and families throughout Switzerland and France. She speaks and writes in English and Spanish fluently, knows conversational French, some Japanese, and basic German.